Claude Debussy

Titles in the series Critical Lives present the work of leading cultural figures of the modern period. Each book explores the life of the artist, writer, philosopher or architect in question and relates it to their major works.

In the same series

Jean Genet
Stephen Barber

Michel Foucault
David Macey

Pablo Picasso
Mary Ann Caws

Franz Kafka
Sander L. Gilman

Guy Debord
Andy Merrifield

Marcel Duchamp
Caroline Cros

James Joyce
Andrew Gibson

Frank Lloyd Wright
Robert McCarter

Jean-Paul Sartre
Andrew Leak

Noam Chomsky
Wolfgang B. Sperlich

Jorge Luis Borges
Jason Wilson

Erik Satie
Mary E. Davis

Georges Bataille
Stuart Kendall

Ludwig Wittgenstein
Edward Kanterian

Octavio Paz
Nick Caistor

Walter Benjamin
Esther Leslie

Charles Baudelaire
Rosemary Lloyd

Jean Cocteau
James S. Williams

Sergei Eisenstein
Mike O'Mahony

Salvador Dalí
Mary Ann Caws

Simone de Beauvoir
Ursula Tidd

Edgar Allan Poe
Kevin J. Hayes

Gertrude Stein
Lucy Daniel

Pablo Neruda
Dominic Moran

Samuel Beckett
Andrew Gibson

William S. Burroughs
Phil Baker

Stéphane Mallarmé
Roger Pearson

Constantin Brancusi
Sanda Miller

Vladimir Nabokov
Barbara Wyllie

Claude Debussy

David J. Code

REAKTION BOOKS

For Nic, for being there

Published by Reaktion Books Ltd
33 Great Sutton Street
London EC1V 0DX, UK

www.reaktionbooks.co.uk

First published 2010

Printed and bound in Great Britain
by Cromwell Press Group, Trowbridge, Wiltshire

British Library Cataloguing in Publication Data
Code, David J.
Claude Debussy. – (Critical lives)
1. Debussy, Claude, 1862-1918
2. Composers—France—Biography
I. Title II. Series
780.9'2-DC22

ISBN: 978 1 86189759 6

Contents

Debussy, watercolour portrait by Paul Robier.

Introduction

A brief glance at the map of Paris discerns some characteristic acumen behind the location of the rue Claude-Debussy in the city's north-western seventeenth arrondissement. Only a few steps away from the junction of this short thoroughfare with the Place de la Porte Champêtre, opening from another *place* named for the American symbolist poet Stuart Merrill, a broader avenue bears the name of Merrill's far more influential teacher, Stéphane Mallarmé. Here is a near-juxtaposition Debussy would surely have appreciated. Like all composers who passed through the Paris Conservatoire he was trained to aspire to the literary-musical hybrid of opera as the pre-eminent genre. But it was through his intensive readings of contemporary poets, from Théodore de Banville and Dante Gabriel Rossetti through Charles Baudelaire, Paul Verlaine and Stéphane Mallarmé, that he primarily refined the literary sensibility that was to render him one of the finest musical readers of poetic and dramatic language. And it was through close collaboration with Mallarmé in particular, in the years around his thirtieth birthday, that this sensibility first achieved the extraordinary sophistication – as exemplified in the *Prélude à l'après-midi d'un faune* – that was to secure him the pivotal place he now occupies in all histories of modern composition.

Perhaps the position of the rue Debussy gives clear evidence that the composer's ties to what is generally termed the Symbolist movement in literature are by now firmly established. But the fact that the Parisian planners chose to emphasize this particular affinity remains worthy of note. From countless CD inserts, sheet music covers and popular music histories, it seems the ostensible links between Debussy's music and the painterly aesthetic of Claude Monet (to give one example) have lodged more solidly in the cultural imagination, leaving Debussy stuck with the label of pre-eminent musical Impressionist. Given that all such '-isms' tend to obscure at least as much as they illuminate, it is useless to argue in general terms for the validity of any one over any other. But while it seems unlikely that this one can ever be dislodged – these days, to compose in an 'Impressionist' manner means simply to compose somewhat like Debussy – there may still be some value in consciously considering the distortions it can impose over an encounter with the oeuvre.

One vivid example of such distortion can be found by setting out from Debussy's last home on the Avenue du Bois de Boulogne in the sixteenth arrondissement and wandering south-west, towards the Bois, about the same distance that would take the proverbial crow (flying north) to the rue Claude-Debussy. This, in fact, was a journey he often took, as he noted with characteristic flippancy during one of many periods of creative frustration:

> Music is sometimes malicious, even to those who love it the most! Thus, I take my daughter and my hat, and I go for a walk in the Bois de Boulogne, where one meets people who have come from very far away in order to be bored in Paris![1]

These days, those who cross the Boulevard Lannes towards the Périphérique and the first line of trees beyond will discover, within the small square identified as the Jardin Claude Debussy, a much more striking memorial to the composer than that drab bit of road up in the seventeenth.

The 1932 monument to Debussy by the Art Deco sculptors Jan and Joël Martel, in the Jardin Claude Debussy in Paris.

At once tomb, temple and triumphal arch, to borrow the words of Émile Vuillermoz (an editor of Debussy's journalism, and a member of the memorial committee), this elaborate monument by the art deco sculptors Jan and Joël Martel faces visitors to the Jardin from the back of a long basin bordered by rosebushes. Its large central panel, carved with a bas-relief of imagery associated with Debussy's works, is flanked by sculpted nymph-musicians atop side-panels bearing a dedication that invokes the patriotic signature he adopted late in life: '*À Claude Debussy / Musicien Français*'. These are the only words visible from the front. But to step around to the back is to discover more textual apparatus accompanying another relief of the composer at the piano before a tableau of musicians. A phrase Debussy once attributed to his critical alter-ego 'Monsieur Croche' – 'it is necessary to seek for discipline in liberty, to listen for advice from no-one except the wind that passes, telling us the history of the world' – and a notation of the famous opening flute solo from his Mallarméan *Prélude* sits atop a list of contributors to the monument; a list of works fills the panels beneath the nymphs.[2]

Nowhere do these blocks of text mention Impressionism or Symbolism. But while the musical excerpt seems to reaffirm the literary affinity inscribed into the city's streets, the terms in which Vuillermoz, for one, noted his approval of the design exemplify just how firmly the painterly label, instead, had become fixed by the dedication in 1932:

> This monument . . . eternalizes . . . the love that the Impressionist master had for the reflections in the water, the clouds, the flowers, the leaves and the branches. It is reflected in the crystal mirror of a basin that evokes that of the *Promenoir des Deux Amants*. Two sheets of shimmering water emerge to ripple beneath the feet of the musician-naïads. The quivering foliage of the Bois de Boulogne just alongside will murmur the infinite melody that Debussy loved to listen to and to draw into the great universal symphony of nature. This was indeed the perfect way to commemorate the genius of a poet of timbres and a painter of sounds.[3]

While the last pairing – 'poet' and 'painter' – seems reasonably balanced, the nature imagery earlier in the paragraph is tellingly selective. 'Reflections in the water' and 'Clouds' both name Debussy works that could well be heard as tone paintings (*Reflets dans l'eau* from the *Images* for piano; *Nuages* from the *Nocturnes* for orchestra). But each belongs to a triptych that also includes more culturally invested evocations: *Hommage à Rameau* in the *Images*; *Fêtes* and *Sirènes* in the *Nocturnes*. The rest of the list – 'the flowers, the leaves, and the branches' – is even more blatantly severed from its context in Verlaine's poem 'Green': 'Here are the fruits, the flowers, the leaves, and the branches, / And here is my heart, which beats only for you.' No simple nature painting, Debussy's early setting of this poem revisits the pastoral trope of natural abundance as a token of passion. Perhaps Vuillermoz restores some explicit literary inflection when he lets the 'crystal mirror' of the basin inspire a nod to the late song triptych *Le Promenoir des deux amants*. But in this case, he isolates some background scenery from a set of three poems Debussy carved out of a larger, seventeenth-century original in order to trace delicately poised stages of intimacy between two lovers.

If this one paragraph perfectly exemplifies the tendency, under the Impressionist cliché, to underplay the degree to which Debussy's 'representational' music taps timeless humane concerns (cultural identity; desire; lyrical expression; intimacy), the monument that inspired it can actually be seen to suggest a more appropriate approach. To be sure, the Martel brothers include plenty of leaves, clouds and water in the background of their central panel. But they give central importance to a column of figures taken from three ambitious compositional readings. At bottom right a disrobing nymph glances up to meet the lustful eyes of a flute-playing faun. Just above, the young Pelléas luxuriates in the tresses of his brother's wife, Mélisande, as she leans from her tower window. And atop the relief, a haloed androgynous figure shows the Christ-like Saint Sebastian, who was martyred by his own archers for refusing to foreswear his faith.

References to other works fall into secondary positions around these evocations of exceptional Debussyan readings from three decades: the Mallarmé *Prélude* (1894); the Maeterlinck opera *Pelléas et Mélisande* (1902); and the quasi-religious 'mystery' on a text by Gabriele d'Annunzio, *Le Martyre de Saint-Sébastien* (1911). If the status of the third of these works remains more contested than the other two, and if the literary tower is missing a foundation in the decade in which Debussy first found his voice as a musical reader, the bas-relief nonetheless offers a salutary summons to anyone who wishes to hear more than a 'symphony of nature' in his music. In other words, a critical biography might well draw on the same structural insight as the Martel twins, and restore Debussy's readerly acuity to the centre of his oeuvre – not just by reappraising the musical poetry in such works as the *Prélude* and *Pelléas*, but also by considering how that poetic sensibility radiated out into works of less obvious literary affinity.

It remains to consider how this artistic sensibility might relate to the life represented, on the back of the monument, by that figure at the piano. Here again, the focus on Debussy as reader can be of help, if only to note that the occasions of his song-writing occasionally bore some direct relationship to the vagaries of his personal life. The fact that he was a pianist, too, is clearly of significance. Although he failed by the Conservatoire's implacable measures to attain official virtuoso status, his creative engagement with the instrument was to prove a crucial resource in years of penury, and a fertile means to explore the relationship between esoteric and public pleasures at a pivotal moment in the history of modern music. Perhaps, to recall the words of 'Monsieur Croche' on the monument, this is a limited way to inscribe his life and work within 'the history of the world'. But in a wider view, any consideration of Debussy's formative immersion in the richly allegorical writings of Baudelaire and Mallarmé brings with it questions about the degree to which his music, like their poetry, might embody oblique reflections on the experience of nascent modernity in *fin-de-siècle* France.

The following chapters, in retracing those events from the life that seem most crucial to an understanding of Debussy the man, will try to demonstrate through selective examples how even a partial appreciation of the layers of poetic and allegorical meaning in his works requires a willingness to listen to them with close, readerly attention. Such a suggestion may fly in the face of his occasional breezy claims to an ideal of expressive simplicity. But one subsidiary theme of any Debussy biography will inevitably be the unreliable, contradictory guidance he left us about his artistic ambitions. Even the nationalistic signature '*musicien français*' that now runs across the Martel monument can only seem a slightly deceptive rhetorical gesture in light of the diverse influences that actually combined to forge this 'French' musical voice, which may have indulged in patriotic bombast on one or two occasions but more often sought to evoke what Debussy once called 'an imaginary country, forever impossible to locate'.[4]

Debussy's house of birth at 38 rue au Pain, Saint-Germain-en-Laye, now the Musée Claude Debussy.

1

A Music that Clothes the Poetry

Childhood and First Musical Steps

It might seem logical to begin a search for the roots of Debussy's literary and musical inclinations by taking a short RER trip to Saint-Germain-en-Laye, tucked in a broad loop of the Seine about a dozen miles north-west of Paris. Birthplace of three French kings, including the 'Sun King' Louis XIV himself, this rather grand suburb today houses in a seventeenth-century house at 38 rue au Pain both the offices of the tourist board and the numerous photographs, documents and *objets d'art* that make up the Musée Claude Debussy. It was in this same house that a first son, christened Achille-Claude, was born on 22 August 1862 to the struggling proprietors of a china shop, Manuel and Victorine Debussy.

The fact of birth aside, however, it is doubtful whether the air of this elegant suburb retains much trace of the atmosphere that first nourished an artistic sensibility. In truth, a seeker after those originary scents might do better, first of all, to return to the metropolis and walk the streets of the Clichy district where, their shopkeeping venture having failed, the family (augmented by a daughter Adèle in 1863) moved two years after the birth of their eldest child. And then, after following the Debussys (joined by a second son, Emmanuel, in 1867) on a further move in 1868 to 69 rue St.-Honoré, not far from Manuel's latest employment at a printing company in the Magasins du Louvre, our seeker could

Achille-Claude Debussy at the age of five.

perhaps be persuaded to attempt a longer jaunt to Cannes in the sunny south, where, during a stay with his mother's sister Clémentine some time in 1870 or 1871, music first entered the life of Achille-Claude.

Apparently it was Debussy's aunt Clémentine who 'had the strange idea' of getting him to learn piano, which he began to do, first of all, with an 'old Italian professor named Cerutti' – in fact, as later biographers have established, a violinist in his early forties then resident in Cannes.[1] These first ventures showed promise enough that the family began entertaining the possibility of an alternative career for Achille than that initially envisioned as a sailor. The next step in the unfolding of that career arose, ironically, from the misfortune of his father back in Paris. While imprisoned for his participation in the battles of the Commune against the Thiers government, Manuel Debussy met the *communard* composer of operettas and popular songs Charles de Sivry. On hearing of young Achille-Claude's musical gifts, de Sivry recommended as a piano teacher his own mother, Antoinette Mauté.

The jury remains out regarding the precise shades of half-truth in Mme Mauté's claim to be a piano student of Frédéric Chopin.[2] But whatever pedigree stood behind her methods, they were remarkably successful in nurturing Debussy's raw talents, over little more than a year, to the point at which he could present himself in 1872 for admission to the Paris Conservatoire. Whether or not his success in securing one of the 33 places granted to the 157 applicants had something to do with a supporting letter his father obtained from the senior composer Félicien David, it was with dreams of a virtuoso career that the ten-year-old Debussy first entered the most renowned institution of musical and dramatic education in France.[3]

While it is easy enough to 'join the dots' from Debussy's early childhood to this entry into professional musical instruction – a solicitous aunt; a first stab at musical rudiments with a jobbing violinist; a fortuitous introduction to an inspiring teacher – the sources of his literary affinities have proven harder to trace. The oft-noted fact that he received no official education prior to his studies at the Conservatoire was, in truth, hardly exceptional, for compulsory childhood education would not be introduced in France until 1881–2, with the passing of the so-called 'Jules Ferry laws' (named for the reforming Minister of Education and Prime Minister). About the family environment in which most early education must have taken place we know very little. Manuel's enthusiasm for the operetta of Offenbach may have smoothed his contact with de Sivry but hardly prefigured his son's musical ideals; Victorine's aesthetic inclinations remain unknown. Still, evidence of a home environment hospitable to the seeds of erudition might be extrapolated from the fact that the youngest surviving son, Alfred (born 1870) later published a translation of a different work, 'The Staff and Scrip', by the same Pre-Raphaelite poet, Dante Gabriel Rossetti, whose poem 'The Blessed Damozel' would be set by his brother in the early cantata *La Damoiselle élue*.[4]

The most tantalizing hint of early literary stimulus must again be located in the person of Mme Mauté, Debussy's piano teacher, who was also the mother-in-law of Paul Verlaine – the one poet the composer, in his mature years, would most often set to music. Exactly at the time of Debussy's piano lessons Verlaine was living with his new wife, Mathilde, in her mother's apartment at 14 rue Nicolet, a few blocks from the Debussy household at 59 bis rue Pigalle. Still, no-one has found evidence of contact between poet and young pianist – let alone of any awareness on the latter's part of the torments Mathilde Verlaine was to suffer with the advent of Arthur Rimbaud into her husband's life in late 1871. At any rate, not long after that infamous *fin-de-siècle* literary couple began its extended spiral into tragedy by decamping to London in September 1872, Debussy left the first stage of his studies behind when he joined the piano class of the respected Conservatoire professor Antoine Marmontel.

Conservatoire 1: Failure as a Pianist

The reminiscences that have come to us from Debussy's student colleagues portray an eccentric, clumsy figure, with a habit of arriving late and breathless at Marmontel's thrice-weekly piano classes and playing in a bizarre, forced manner.[5] Within a year or two Marmontel seems to have had some success in bringing this wildness under control, as evidenced by his reports on his pupil's 'true artistic temperament . . . with a promising future'.[6] As if to confirm this prediction, Debussy began to attain success on the long ladder of awards with which the Conservatoire, through annual competitions, marked the progression of its charges.

The piano competitions began well enough, when a 'second certificate of merit' was awarded to the performance of Chopin's F minor concerto in 1874. But Debussy's greater success, at this point, came with a 'third medal' in *solfège*, his second main course of study. Essentially, *solfège* (like the 'tonic *sol-fa*' method familiar from '*Doh*, a deer' in *The Sound of Music*) refers to the principle of assigning syllables to musical pitches to facilitate sight-singing. But the rigorous Conservatoire course extended far beyond singing exercises to embrace a panoply of 'aural gymnastics' whose value to Debussy's development has been argued by one of his classmates, Maurice Emmanuel:

> There is no more effective assistant, for the creative imagination, particularly if it is a quick-witted one, than the instantaneous analysis – honed to an effortless facility – of a harmonic combination of sounds, however complex it may be. Because that immediacy of perception has as a corollary a faculty of mental representation that permits the musician to 'hear,' without actually producing, the sound that he imagines.[7]

Emmanuel further notes how fortunate Debussy was in his teacher of this ostensibly dry subject. Apparently Albert Lavignac (then only 27 years old, and a recent appointment) recognized a gifted pupil's exceptional interest in exercises that discouraged most others and 'let him run ahead' of the course as he searched in new chordal combinations for 'true emotions'. Lavignac further assisted Debussy by guiding him to compositional models that could best support such a search: at one point, teacher and student became so involved in a read-through of Wagner's opera *Tannhäuser* at the piano that they had to stumble out through the darkened Conservatoire after it had officially closed for the night.[8]

The combination of native gifts and Lavignac's guidance lifted Debussy quickly up this particular ladder, to a 'first medal' in *solfège* in 1876. But the piano competitions did not proceed as smoothly. 1875 saw a single upward step, with a 'first certificate of merit'; in January of the following year, a first recorded public appearance at a typical *fin-de-siècle* '*concert-spectacle*' in the town of Chauny (accompanying a singer and a cellist, and playing in a Haydn piano trio) saw the thirteen-year-old hailed as a prodigy.[9] But although a 'second medal' in piano, won in 1877 after failure to gain any award in 1876, may have seemed to re-establish the desired ascent, it was not to be followed by further success in 1878 and 1879. Such failure effectively marked the end of Debussy's ambitions as a professional virtuoso.

From late November 1877, Debussy had also begun attending the harmony class of Émile Durand, author of an important harmony textbook, and described by Emmanuel as the 'dullest of pedagogues'.[10] There is no doubt that Debussy chafed under Durand's strictures: years later, he would disdain textbook harmony for 'unifying musical writing to the point that all musicians, with very few exceptions, harmonize in the same manner'.[11] But by some accounts, Durand was able to express bemused interest in the unorthodox experiments of this student.[12] And on the evidence of an offhand remark later reported by Emmanuel – 'I don't write in the fugal style because I know it' – Debussy was well aware that his flouting of conventions was built on secure foundations.[13] His appreciation for the assistance of this 'dullest' of harmony teachers in securing those foundations can be deduced from the amicable dedication to Durand of his first large-scale composition, the *Piano Trio in G major* of 1880.

Conservatoire II: The Compositional Vocation

The fact that the eighteen-year-old Debussy saw fit to complete the ample four-movement structure of this trio (published in a modern edition in 1986) testifies to the conviction with which, at the end of the 1870s, he turned from his dreams of a piano career to a new, compositional vocation. Some of the impetus for this decision can be located outside the Conservatoire, in a series of performing positions Debussy undertook even as his dreams of official prizes came to nothing. First, Marmontel secured him a summer placement playing piano at the splendid sixteenth-century castle of Chenonceaux in the Loire valley, which had been purchased by the wealthy Scottish engineer Daniel Wilson as a gift for his daughter.

With Marguerite Pelouze-Wilson, his employer through the summer of 1879, Debussy encountered a particularly colourful example of well-heeled artistic obsession. There is cause to believe that each of her three passions – Flaubert's writing, Italian painting and the music of Wagner – left a trace on his developing aesthetic. Debussy would later single out Flaubert as a favourite prose author; one of his early works, *Printemps*, would be inspired by Botticelli's *Primavera*. But the more significant impact undoubtedly came from Mme Pelouze-Wilson's fervid advocacy of Wagner. Along with such leading *wagnéristes* as the composers Vincent d'Indy and Augusta Holmès, she had been part of the small group of 'pilgrims' from France to Bayreuth for the inauguration of the Bayreuth Festspielhaus in 1876; she would repeat the same pilgrimage for five years in succession even as she dissipated her fortune in grand parties and decorative projects. As biographer François Lesure has suggested, it is hard to imagine that this enthusiasm, encountered at white heat by a young musician already drawn into the Wagnerian orbit by his explorations with Lavignac, would not have played a key role in consolidating his new vocation.[14]

The initial fruits of the new vocation were slender enough: according to the reminiscences of a student colleague Paul Vidal, Debussy's first compositions, the songs 'Madrid' and 'Ballade à la lune', can be dated to late 1879.[15] While it is at least worthy of note that Debussy began his career with song-writing, little in the fragments that remain of these settings of Alfred de Musset's Romantic poetry is particularly prophetic of future exquisite musical readings.[16] Meanwhile, on the official side of things, Debussy found himself up against another of the Conservatoire's rules. Entry to a composition class required a first prize in one of the officially recognized 'theory' classes. After two years with Durand, it would have been clear how unlikely he was to gain any such honour in the realm of harmony. His decision to enrol in the accompaniment class of Auguste-Ernest Bazille, on the other hand, quickly led to the required result.

Here again, in this organist and former singing coach at the Opéra-Comique Debussy seems to have found a teacher willing to tolerate a certain amount of idiosyncrasy in a student who demonstrated 'great facility' along with 'initiative and verve'.[17] And here again (as Emmanuel insisted) the dry label 'accompanying' belies the value of a course whose rigour and range, under Bazille's tutelage – the improvisation of accompanying parts to a bass line or melody; the transposition at sight of contemporary works; the pianistic realization of complex orchestral scores – can well be described as a 'progression towards an integrally acquired *métier*'.[18] Debussy's first prize, in 1880, sign of such a fluent, integrated *métier*, opened the door to further study in composition.

But first, another summer abroad intervened. This time, Marmontel recommended him to the rich Russian widow Nadezhda Filaretovna von Meck, who was seeking a piano teacher and vocal accompanist for her children, as well as someone to share at the piano her passion for the music of Tchaikovsky. In July 1880 Debussy joined Mme von Meck's extensive *ménage* of family and servants on one of her habitual peregrinations through European luxury spots – first to Interlachen in Switzerland; then to Arcachon on the French Atlantic coast; finally (via several interim stops) to the opulent Villa Oppenheim in the hills above Florence. Writing to Tchaikovksy (of whom she was a generous supporter) Mme Meck singled out for praise not just the fluent score-reading ability

Nadezhda Filarotevna von Meck, patron of Tchaikovksy, and Debussy's employer for three summers while he was a student at the Paris Conservatoire.

of her Parisian '*gamin*', but also the fact that he was 'delighted' with Tchaikovksy's music.[19] The compliment would not be returned when, having sent Debussy's *Danse bohémienne* for piano to her hero, she received by return only a sneer that 'not a single thought is developed to the end, the form is bungled, and there is no unity'.[20]

Besides this little *Danse* (and the four-hand arrangements from *Swan Lake* for Mme von Meck, which apparently gained Debussy a first publication) the more substantial compositional production of this summer was the piano trio Debussy dedicated to Durand, which was written for an ensemble – himself at the piano with two Russian string players – Mme von Meck had set up to play for her every evening in Florence.[21] While undoubtedly light years removed from the fully fledged mastery of, say, Mendelssohn's *Octet* (another chamber composition by a far more precocious teenager), this work gives a pretty good illustration of the 'imagination and verve' Bazille had admired in Debussy's improvisatory explorations. The thematic character of each movement is relatively well defined; the ensemble treated with some flexibility; the inventive approach to traditional forms only slightly marred by a few clumsy seams. Beyond the evidence of imagination and ambition in this one piece of juvenilia it has occasionally proven tempting, in light of Mme von Meck's comment to Tchaikovksy that 'I play [for him] constantly, and everything I play is new to him', to extrapolate a more general significance from the three summers Debussy ultimately spent in this peripatetic entourage.[22] But her uneven appreciation for the most recent music of her own country clouds any assumption about the role of these private audiences in Debussy's discovery of the modern Russian music that was to prove a crucial counterweight to the Wagnerian seductions he had already begun to sense.[23]

A Teacher, a Muse and a Prize

Early in his correspondence with Mme von Meck, Debussy seems to have embroidered his credentials by claiming to be a '*premier prix*' in piano and a composition student of Massenet, the most eminent teacher at the Conservatoire.[24] But after returning to his studies in November 1880 he instead joined the newly established class of Ernest Guiraud, a composer now known primarily for the recitatives he composed to replace the spoken dialogue in Bizet's *Carmen*. Whether we choose to accept Vallas's generous attribution of a 'broad-minded' approach or Emmanuel's accusation of an 'incurable indolence,' Guiraud was to prove a congenial teacher who would shepherd Debussy through his three attempts at the Conservatoire's highest honour, the Prix de Rome, and remain a friend up to his death in 1892.[25]

From the Conservatoire archives it is apparent that Debussy also audited the organ classes of César Franck, then a highly influential figure in the Société Nationale de Musique, founded a decade earlier to foster the revival of French musical pride after the humiliations of the 1870 Franco-Prussian war. Although we might expect Franck's emphasis on improvisation to have had some appeal, Debussy's patience for the Belgian composer's endless 'modulations' (that is, moving from key to key) seems to have quickly worn thin.[26] The more important influence on Debussy around 1880–81 again came from outside the Conservatoire. Although he was still living in the family home, his fondness for books and trinkets demanded a regular income. On the recommendation of Vidal he took up a position as accompanist for a singing school run by a former opera singer, Victorine Moreau-Santi, for young well-to-do women.

Soon enough, in one not-quite-so-young student, Marie Vasnier (the 32-year-old wife of an older 'inspector of buildings' Henri Vasnier), Debussy encountered a woman who would become, over the next few years, both his first significant romantic passion and his first important muse. To be sure, between 1881 and the 1884 Prix de Rome, Debussy spent considerable time on instrumental composition, completing four-hand versions of a *Symphony in B minor* for Mme von Meck (of which only one movement survives) and a few other orchestral works, as well as a *Nocturne et scherzo* for cello and piano. But it was the 23 songs for voice and piano he wrote for Marie Vasnier, along with about the same number for other (or unnamed) dedicatees, that offered the most extensive evidence of his developing compositional sensibility and the literary interests that sustained it.

Imprecision about exact dates aside, some general trends can be noted in this evolving literary exploration. First of all, Debussy was much less interested in early Romantic poets than in the more recent work of the Parnassian Théodore de Banville, who received fully twelve settings between 1880 and early 1882 (including Debussy's first published song, 'Nuit d'étoiles'). This particular poetic penchant was to prove beneficial in indirect ways: one of

Paul Baudry's 1882 oil portrait of Marie Vasnier, wife of an important supporter, early love interest and dedicatee of many youthful songs.

the composer's closest friends, Raymond Bonheur – who had come to Durand's harmony class after beginning dramatic studies at the Conservatoire – later recalled that he had first been drawn to Debussy by the extraordinary sight in that context of a volume of Banville in his hand.[27] Amidst the poets he set less often in these years, it is striking to note, alongside the other Parnassian Leconte de Lisle, a writer much closer to Debussy's own generation, Maurice Bouchor (born 1855). Then, from late 1882 onwards, Banville would be put aside as Debussy turned to a first cluster of settings of Verlaine, a single setting of Mallarmé, and no less than eight settings of another nearer contemporary, Paul Bourget (a writer and critic whose enthusiasm for English literature was likely influential on Debussy), composed through late 1883, 1884 and into 1885.[28]

In light of their effusive dedications – for example, 'To Madame Vanier [*sic*], the only muse that has ever inspired me to something resembling a musical sentiment (to speak only of that)' – it is easy to see some of these songs as direct emanations from the love affair with Marie Vasnier.[29] Compositionally, while the earliest songs largely evince a relatively simple, Massenet- or Gounod-inspired lyricism, the first settings of Verlaine (many of which were revised years later) contain more than a hint at the refinement this poet would inspire in the mature Debussy. Still, the most audacious choice for a song lyric was undoubtedly Mallarmé's early poem 'Apparition', whose serpentine, sonorously compacted sentences hardly seem to invite melodic declamation:

La lune s'attristait. Des séraphins en pleurs
Rêvant, l'archet aux doigts, dans le calme des fleurs
Vaporeuses, tiraient de mourantes violes
De blancs sanglots glissant sur l'azur des corolles.

[The moon was grieving. Seraphim in tears / Dreaming, bow in hand, in the calm of vaporous / Flowers, drew from faltering viols / White sobs sliding over the blue of corollas.]

Debussy's 1884 setting of these arch-Symbolist lines begins with some anticipation of the delicacies and depths the same writer was to inspire a decade later in the *Prélude à l'après-midi d'un faune*. Indeed, some characteristic inflections of his song style are already audible in the dreamy, one-note incantation of the first three words over delicately oscillating accompaniment (though the full-blooded *salon* lyricism that launches the second stanza – 'It was the blessed day of your first kiss' – is less prophetic).

Besides the liaison with Marie Vasner – and indeed, with the whole Vasnier household, which became a second Parisian home for Debussy – the years 1880–82 had also seen further travels with Mme von Meck. The summer of 1881 had begun with a first trip to Russia. For two months the family was largely based in Moscow, but it seems Debussy joined them on at least one trip to the grand estate of Mme von Meck's daughter at Gourievo.[30] Subsequently, Mme Meck's travels during October and November again brought him to several great European cities – Vienna and Trieste, Venice and Rome – before the entourage settled again, briefly, in Florence. A particularly late return to his studies met with the censure of Guiraud, in spite of Debussy's dedication to his teacher of one recent composition (an *Ouverture Diane*). Nonetheless, his newfound compositional fluency seems to have given him enough confidence to attempt, for the first time, the preliminary test for entry to the Prix de Rome competition.

The four-voice fugue and choral work ('Salut, printemps') written for this first attempt did not win Debussy through to the official competition. Undeterred, he proceeded to draft a series of works through the spring and summer of 1882 (including further piano pieces inspired by Banville, and a cantata *Daniel*), before tearing himself away from the Vasniers' summer villa in Ville d'Avray for a third and last summer sojourn with Mme von Meck, now at her estate outside Moscow. The most significant musical discovery, this time, was likely the songs of Balakirev, which she praised to Tchaikovksy not only for their 'picturesque character, which speaks to the imagination' but also for the way their melodic line 'detaches itself against a distinct background'.[31] It could be that this latest Russian musical inspiration conjoined with the latest poetic discovery in securing the artistic advance in the Verlaine settings 'En sourdine' and 'Mandoline' Debussy brought back from Russia. Another late return to Guiraud's class found the teacher newly back from Bayreuth, annoyed at the quasi-religious fervour he had encountered – 'If only you knew how terrible these Wagnerians are!' he complained to one correspondent, 'even enthusiasm is frowned upon . . . only ecstasy is tolerated' – but bowled over by the 'beauties of the highest order' in Wagner's last opera, *Parsifal*.[32] But of Debussy's reactions to Guiraud's reports of a work that would remain, with *Tristan und Isolde*, a central touchstone of his own ambitions we unfortunately know nothing.

In the spring of the same year, in the face of a report from Guiraud that accused him of 'writing music badly', Debussy first attempted a setting of a dramatic work by Banville, the 'heroic comedy' *Diane au bois*.[33] But Guiraud was quick to dissuade him from this idiosyncratic venture in view of the more pressing need to confront again the test for the Prix de Rome competition. This time, Debussy's fugue and choral setting of Lamartine's 'Invocation' won him through to the competition proper. As was customary, the five finalists were provided with a text for a cantata – *Le gladiateur* by Emile Moreau – and housed in the Château de Compiègne just outside Paris for 25 days to compose. When the resulting works were performed before the Institut, the first prize was promptly given to Debussy's friend Paul Vidal. After lengthy debate, the jury awarded the second prize to Debussy. (Some critics agreed, but at least one recognized in his work the 'most original personality'.[34]) Debussy was gracious enough in defeat to invite Guiraud and Vidal to a celebratory meal with his family, who fêted Vidal as warmly as if he were one of their own children.[35]

Another paid appointment was the indirect result of the failure to win top prize, for when Vidal left for the Rome residency that came with his victory he put Debussy forward to replace him as the regular accompanist for an amateur choral society. It is clear from his letters of excuse to the choir's director that Debussy was not diligent in his attendance at weekly rehearsals. But he did enough to hold onto a position that, beyond supplementing the wages he was still receiving from Mme Moreau-Santi, also involved him in the preparation of a vast range of choral repertoire extending from Palestrina to Gounod via Bach, Mozart, Mendelssohn and Liszt. Such hands-on experience was undoubtedly of value as he approached, again, the last rung on the Conservatoire's ladder to success – especially in light of the vivid accounts we

Marcel Baschet's 1884 pastel portrait of Debussy: the composer as Prix de Rome laureate.

have received of his growing tendency, during the last year of study, to entertain his peers with impishly rebellious improvisations.[36]

Guiraud managed to tame such indulgences enough for Debussy to make it through the initial tests and into the Château de Compiègne, again, as one of the five finalists for the 1884 Prix de Rome. This time, his three weeks of work on the cantata *L'Enfant prodigue*, with a text by Édouard Guinand, saw him crowned with the first grand prize. Many have seen this success as the result of a deliberate prize-winning strategy of conformance to official expectations; indeed Debussy himself noted, on returning to the cantata years later, the corrections needed to remove its odour of 'the Conservatoire, and boredom'.[37] But however clear its debts to Gounod and Massenet may be, *L'Enfant prodigue* nonetheless projected enough artistic personality for at least one critic to recognize the refined literary sensibility through the well-mannered veneer. 'In making, so to speak, an abstraction of the assigned text,' A. Héler wrote in *L'Art musical*, '[Debussy] has dared to seek the colour of the poetry.'[38]

Such a response is all the more striking in view of the relatively colourless text Debussy had to work with. The parable in the Gospel of Luke of the father who celebrates the return of his wayward younger son (in spite of the eldest's resentment) was significantly adapted to official purposes by Guinand. Most notably, his addition of the character of Lia, mother of the prodigal son Azaël, to the '*scène lyrique*' he concocted from the biblical original largely dissipates the focus on an act of paternal forgiveness that had inspired, among other things, one of the most touching of Rembrandt's canvasses. The emotional core of Guinand's text becomes, instead, the moment when Lia, bewailing her lost son, belatedly recognizes a 'poor stranger' asleep on a riverbank.

Debussy's treatment of this scene makes the most of what colour there was to find in Guinand's poetry. His progression from delicate orchestral 'light' effects at 'open your eyes' through the swelling sentimentality of the duo 'Fortunate hours' (culminating in the joint pronouncement 'Just like before, gives you her/his love!') demonstrates a fluency with broad emotional strokes, from operatic distress to the passionate warmth of maternal-filial union. But Debussy's ingenuity cannot quite save the first (maternal) moment of forgiveness from seeming a bathetic irrelevance amidst the mutual on-sleeve effusions; the poignancy of a second, paternal bestowal of mercy – already dulled by the faint sense of repetition – is further undermined by Guinand's decision to construct the father, Siméon, as a rather portentous patriarch. Finally, the group genuflection to a beneficent God Guinand tacked on as a finale may have given Debussy a chance to show that his emotional palette extended to tub-thumping joy, but it hardly did much for the humane subtlety of the cantata as a whole.

Whatever its failings, *L'Enfant prodigue* amply demonstrated Debussy's ability to find rich musical equivalents even to poetic colours less congenial than those painted by his preferred verbal artists Banville, Verlaine and Bourget. Still, he seems to have been aware that this last, successful negotiation of the Conservatoire's maze of rules and requirements was only the first step in a long and difficult accommodation of his art to the strictures of French musical officialdom. Years later, he recalled that after the performances of the cantatas he stepped away from the Institut to gaze over the play of sunlight on the Seine from the Pont des Arts. When a colleague broke his reverie to inform him of his success his first feeling was that 'all his joy was over'.[39] His reluctance to abandon Paris and his muse Marie Vasnier for two years is clear from the fact that he delayed his departure for Rome until 28 January 1885 – and thus barely took up his residency before the last possible date (31 January) stipulated by the rules.

When in Rome . . .

The idea that an ambitious young composer might profit from a two-year residency in Rome may seem uncontroversial enough. But it is worth noting that the Prix de Rome had originally been founded (in 1663) out of reverence for the painting, sculpture and architecture of the Italian Renaissance. The 1803 expansion of the prize's remit to include music alongside the three initial fields rested on less solid grounds. Given that Paris, not Rome, was the more vibrant musical centre for a musician of Debussy's ilk, it is easy to understand his resistance to two years of 'imprisonment' in the Villa Médicis. In their endless complaints of tedium and inability to work, and their melodramatic comparisons of the Villa and its directors to a prison and its gaolers, the letters he wrote to Paris throughout the first months of his residency prove, at times, rather tedious reading themselves. But they also hold forth intriguing glimmers of the particularly exacting aesthetic inclinations that were to nourish his mature style.

Henri Vasnier, the recipient of many plaintive missives, was to prove a particularly important supporter through these years. It was Vasnier who dissuaded Debussy more than once from giving up on the hated residency, with its requirement of a series of works, or *envois*, to be submitted yearly to the Institut des Beaux-Arts in Paris. And it was to Vasnier that Debussy offered this candid glimpse of his compositional vision as he wrestled with the 'great, idiotic verses' of his first *envoi*, *Zuléïma*, based on a French adaptation of Heinrich Heine's Spanish-themed historical ballad *Almansor*:

> I believe that I will never be able to enclose my music within an overly rigid mould – I hasten to say that I am not speaking of musical form, but simply from a literary perspective. I would much prefer the kind of thing in which, so to speak, the action will be sacrificed to a deliberately pursued expression of the sentiments of the soul, it seems to me that in that case music could make itself more human, more like lived experience, and that one could hollow out [*creuser*] and refine the means of delivery.[40]

Not only would the emphasis, here, on the 'literary perspective' recur again and again in these letters, but the final turn of phrase, echoing Mallarmé's obsessive desire to '*creuser le vers*' (hollow out the poetic verse), underlines the aesthetic affinity dimly exemplified in the recent setting of 'Apparition'.[41] Already, Debussy is envisioning a music of extreme literary refinement, and a 'hollowing out' of aesthetic means, based not on any wilful urge to preciosity but rather on an ideal of the most 'human' expression of lived emotional experience.

Mallarméan glimmers aside, at this early age Debussy's 'literary perspective' clearly admitted of other, equally strong beacons of influence. For one thing, the similar ideal he expressed (in a slightly later letter to Vasnier) of a music 'supple enough, forceful enough, to adapt itself to the lyrical movements of the soul and the caprices of dreams', echoes the preface to Charles Baudelaire's collection *Petits Poèmes en Prose* so closely as to read like a misremembered quotation.[42] And as Debussy wearily testified to the intractable nature of *Zuléïma* (which would be submitted, to withering critique, but subsequently lost) he also returned again and again to discuss similar struggles with Banville's *Diane au bois,* a text whose greater appeal was due in some part to the fact that it 'did not in the slightest recall the kind of poems that usually served for an *envoi*'.[43]

Although his setting of *Diane au bois* was to remain incomplete, we owe to these more personally invested toils several further succinct expressions of distinctive ambitions as a musical reader. Vasnier, again, would receive a letter on the subject of *Diane* complaining of a 'difficulty of inserting into as clear a form as possible the thousand sensations of a character'.[44] But it was to Claudius Popelin, the father of one of Debussy's comrades at the Villa, that he scribbled one of the pithiest images of all. Rejecting a conventional approach to music for the theatre, Debussy claims to Popelin, in late 1885, to be seeking 'a music that, in a sense, clothes the poetry, to convey the sensation of something truly lived'.[45]

For all its frustrations, the Rome sojourn thus offered Debussy valuable time to temper his aesthetic ambitions. But any urge to seek inspiration from the artistic riches on offer just outside the

Villa seems to have been short-lived. A letter of early 1885 expressed Debussy's awe before Michelangelo – 'the modern pushed to its ultimate limit' – but soon enough, after the first of many brief escapes to Paris, he was describing himself as 'a man whom one drags to the Sistine chapel as if to the scaffold'.[46] As he agonized between *Zuléïma* and *Diane au bois* over the ensuing months, the efforts of the new director Hébert and his wife to enliven his stay with cultural excursions only rendered the residency rather more 'odious' to him than it already was.[47] By autumn, he was still threatening demission, having temporarily lost the compositional facility he had so recently possessed.

Musical inspiration was not wholly lacking. Debussy was often called on to play at the Héberts' social engagements – at times with Vidal (Wagnerian explorations continued in four-hand performances of *Die Meistersinger* and *Parsifal*); at times accompanying Hébert in Mozart's violin sonatas; at times presenting his own most recent songs. An experience of the Renaissance counterpoint of Palestrina sung in a small, plain church reawakened the ideal of musical-verbal alchemy: this music, Debussy enthused, 'underlines the sentiment of the words with an unheard-of profundity, and occasionally, there are certain unrollings of melodic design that convey the effect of illuminations of ancient missals'.[48] In January 1886, a more up-to-date inspiration arrived at the Villa in the person of the elderly Franz Liszt. The visit may not have begun on the most auspicious note: as Vidal reported, Liszt fell asleep during a performance of his *Faust Symphony* on two pianos by himself and Debussy. Undeterred, they also performed for him the next day, and were in the audience when he returned to the Villa to perform three of his own pieces a few days later.[49] The experience left Debussy with a lifelong memory of Liszt's distinctive pedalling technique, which he described years later as 'a kind of breathing'.[50]

Around the same time, the most recent Prix de Rome laureate, Xavier Leroux, arrived to become with Debussy and Vidal an 'inseparable trio' who whiled away afternoons deciphering Bach's organ works and reciting Shakespeare and Banville.[51] But such congenial interactions in the Villa aside, it is clear that Debussy's aesthetic compass was still oriented towards Paris. The later months of 1886 brought into view a new metropolitan correspondent in the person of Émile Baron, bookseller in the rue de Rome. The letters to Baron (which began, in September 1886, with the cry 'I want to see some Manet! And hear some Offenbach!') are filled with requests for books by various Symbolist authors – Moréas; Verlaine; Vignier; Morice; Huysmans – as well as for issues of the numerous journals that proliferated, at the time, in Parisian artistic circles.[52] In light of this further evidence of voracious, up-to-date literary interest, it is surprising that Debussy, having abandoned *Diane au bois*, chose for his second *envoi* a textless 'symphonic suite' for orchestra and wordless chorus.

Describing this latest work, *Printemps*, in a letter to Baron Debussy took pains to distance it from any literary programme:

> I wanted to express the slow and difficult genesis of beings and things in nature, then the expansive blossoming that culminates in an explosive joy at being reborn to a new life, so to speak; all this of course without programme, having a profound disdain for music that is forced to follow some short literary work which is solicitously provided to the audience on entering.[53]

Such disdain for music based on a 'short literary work' reads strangely in retrospect given the refinement Debussy would produce half a dozen years later in his orchestral reading of Mallarmé's 110-line poem *L'après-midi d'un faune*. More immediately, while Debussy had also sought to avoid simple pictorialism (the title, he claimed, should not imply a portrayal of spring 'in the descriptive sense' but rather 'from the human perspective'), one unfortunate result of the second *envoi* was to be the first documented appearance of the 'Impressionist' label that subsequently proved impossible to dislodge. Debussy's 'feeling for musical colour is so strong that he is apt to forget the importance of accuracy of line and form', asserted the official report on *Printemps*. 'He should beware of this vague impressionism which is one of the most dangerous enemies of artistic truth.'[54]

Deceptive as it may be for the mature oeuvre, this first, critical invocation of 'impressionism' was arguably a reasonable response to *Printemps*. Given that Debussy did not actually complete the *envoi* – he sent a partially orchestrated version, with a lame excuse about the loss of the score in a fire – we know it now through a much later version completed in collaboration with the younger composer Henri Busser. Still, it is easy enough to understand why this continuous proliferation of vaguely interrelated thematic wisps across an awkwardly balanced two-movement form drew criticism for amorphousness. Perhaps Debussy over-reached himself in his desire, as he put it, 'to give the most sensations possible'.[55] Or perhaps the grand canvas that stands behind this piece, with its allegorical portrayal of Aphrodite and Cupid surrounded by Flora, Zephyr and Mercury (among others), proved so capacious an inspiration that Debussy's music – which would later generally show meticulous formal control – could only devolve into a diffuseness that ironically summoned reference to a pictorial aesthetic radically different from Botticelli's.

Back to Paris

Printemps would prove the last of the *envois* actually composed in Rome, for in early 1887 Debussy left the Villa Medici for the last time. Ironically, a first letter back to Hébert invoked the residency with wistful nostalgia in the face of his peers' more rapid achievements in the Parisian 'bazaar of success'. But the same letter noted

Honoré Daumier's 1868 caricature of typical *wagnériste* passions: 'IN MUNICH: After a solid hour of Wagner!!'

an intense re-engagement with Parisian culture. On the musical side, a mixed orchestral programme at the Concerts Lamoureux inspired Debussy to single out Wagner's *Tristan und Isolde* as 'the most beautiful work that I know, from the point of view of the depth of the emotion, which embraces you like a caress, makes you suffer'. On the literary side, a new production of *Hamlet*, with the renowned actor Mounet-Sully, struck him as 'just as beautiful as ever'.[56]

Not long after Debussy's return, the affair with Marie Vasnier seems to have run its course. But at the same time, Debussy began to find, or re-establish, friendships that would prove singularly important through his early career and beyond. The younger composer Paul Dukas was to prove particularly valued company for his similar musical enthusiasms and a literary erudition that extended to a shared admiration for Mallarmé. Around the same time Debussy made the acquaintance of an older composer, Ernest Chausson, a well-off student of Franck at the Conservatoire who would become a key supporter over the next few years. The generosity of another wealthy acquaintance, Étienne Dupin, allowed Debussy to take his first pilgrimage to Bayreuth in 1888, where he heard *Parsifal* and *Die Meistersinger*. The opportunity to socialize, on the same trip, with many leading members of the Société Nationale de Musique (which Debussy had officially joined in January) resulted in a written agreement to provide a new orchestral piece for the coming season.[57]

As it turned out, the first music by Debussy to be heard at a Société nationale concert would actually be two of the five Verlaine songs, *Ariettes*, he played with the tenor Maurice Bagès in Februrary 1889. Admirable early exemplars of his mature 'Verlaine style' as these songs may be – revised in 1903 as *Ariettes oubliées*, the set includes 'C'est l'extase langoureuse', one of the most sensuously indulgent of all his songs – they can be seen as less significant in the consolidation of his literary-musical sensibility than two other musical readings that both took longer to find a hearing. The first of these was his third Prix de Rome *envoi,* the cantata *La Damoiselle élue* on Gabriel Sarrazin's translation of Dante Gabriel Rossetti's 'The Blessed Damozel', which was completed and submitted in 1888 but not performed until 1893. The second was a more private venture altogether: the *Cinq Poèmes de Charles Baudelaire,* composed over a year and more before eventually being published, in 1890, in a privately funded luxury edition – and not given a complete public performance until much later.

The choice of a Rossetti poem for the third *envoi* exemplifies the fellow-feeling that flourished, briefly and intensely, between French symbolist and English Pre-Raphaelite circles.[58] Showing some of the care for form and pacing that would later recur in his deft excisions from Maeterlinck's play *Pelléas et Mélisande,* Debussy pared down the poem's 24 strophes to fourteen but retained the basic three-part structure. An opening exchange between Chorus and Narrator presents the eponymous 'blessed damozel' leaning 'from the gold bar of Heaven' amidst rising souls of recently dead lovers; in a lengthy central solo she details her desire to be reunited with her own lover 'to live as once on earth with Love . . . for ever'; a closing return to Chorus and Narrator notes the passing of the light 'fill'd with angels', leaving her alone, face in hands, weeping.

Entering after an introductory series of exquisitely coloured orchestral 'panels', Debussy's four-part female chorus begins its faintly hieratic declamation unaccompanied before proceeding to gather, over time, a richly fluctuating garb of instrumental support. The solo singing generally coils within narrow melodic spans, only occasionally broadening (notably at the damozel's climactic invocation of Love 'for ever') to release a version of the passion once given to Lia in *L'Enfant prodigue*. But the fleeting appearance of such sentimental directness within this more restrained environment only underlines the distance Debussy has travelled between the two cantatas. The precious, mystical imagery of the Pre-Raphaelite text allows for a sublimation of lyrical expression to a higher, more oblique level – as, for example, in the most captivating orchestral swell of the opening choral section, which serves no emotive outburst but rather an eminently Rossettian synaesthetic image: 'Her voice was like the voice the stars had when they sang together.'

Lyrical details aside, the cantata also marked a significant step forward in Debussy's orchestral thinking. To usher in the damozel's solo, for example, a cor anglais passes its lilting melody to an oboe that drifts down to a low note of arrival all-but inaudibly tinted by an added flute. The pale flute hue then hovers briefly in isolation until, after a brief breath of silence, the soprano voice enters ('I wish that he were come to me') and retraces the same line of descent. Similar deft timbral dialogue marks both the end of her long utterance and the end of the entire poem, where, after the last word '*pleura*' (wept), a melody unfurls from cor anglais, to French horn, to harp, before the strings utter a brief, hushed peroration.

Perhaps it was this fine attention to touches of orchestral colour that led the members of the Institut, in revisiting the general thrust of their critique of *Printemps*, to offer a telling new inflection. This music, said the official report on *La Damoiselle élue*, was 'not without poetry or charm, for all that it again feels the effects of those systematic tendencies currently fashionable in artistic expression and form'.[59] The querulous reference to 'systematic tendencies' is striking: these were the years that saw the rise in post-Impressionist circles of the so-called 'pointillist' style – that is, the experiments by Paul Seurat and his followers in the systematic application of discrete touches of complementary colour.[60] But whether or not Debussy would have secretly approved of this implied association of his music with the most up-to-date painterly explorations, his Rossetti cantata would ultimately remain more securely associated with a different strand of post-Impressionism due to the cover later provided for its first edition (1893) by the young painter Maurice Denis. And when asked in 1889 to identify his favourite painters for a questionnaire, Debussy named the quattrocento muse of *Printemps*, Botticelli, along with Gustave Moreau, then an *éminence grise* in Symbolist artistic circles whose paintings of mythological scenes are more akin to the Pre-Raphaelites than to Seurat or Denis.[61]

In the same questionnaire, Debussy singled out Flaubert and Poe as prose authors; Palestrina, Bach and Wagner as composers. But in response to the question about favourite poets he gave only one name: Baudelaire. This response reflects the centrality to his thought, from late 1887 to early 1889, of the monumentally grand *Cinq Poèmes de Charles Baudelaire*, a set of five songs on poems selected from the infamous collection *Les Fleurs du mal*. Given the central role of Baudelaire's writings in the growth of *fin-de-siècle wagnérisme* from its marginal, partisan beginnings in the 1860s to widespread mania in the '80s it is appropriate that some of these songs should feature Debussy's most strenuous dialogues with Wagnerian musical style.[62] Debussy set his seal to this association when, having secured a limited-edition publication through the owner of an occult bookshop, Edmond Bailly, he dedicated the songs to Étienne Dupin – a sponsor of the edition and also of his first trip to Bayreuth in 1888.

Still, while the Wagnerian influence is unmistakable in the uncharacteristically dense, quasi-orchestral writing of some piano parts, the tendency to view these songs from this perspective alone undersells their importance to Debussy's development as a musical reader. One early biographer, Louise Liebich, noted of *La Damoiselle élue* that in spite of its riches, the cantata inevitably lacked any sense of the finely crafted poetic 'charm' of Rossetti's English original.[63] In setting Baudelaire, Debussy now tackled some of the most potent verbal music in French poetry. Of the five poems he selected from *Les Fleurs du mal*, three pose direct challenges to compositional ingenuity in their patterns of textual repetition. The other two are sonnets, no less finely balanced between intensity of lyric utterance and refinement of prosodic craft.

The challenge in the first poem, 'Le Balcon', arises from the self-enclosed, symmetrical structure of each stanza:

Mère des souvenirs, maîtresse des maîtresses,
O toi, tous mes plaisirs! ô toi, tous mes devoirs!
Tu te rappeleras la beauté des caresses,
La douceur du foyer et le charme des soirs,
Mère des souvenirs, maîtresses des maîtresses!

[Mother of memories, mistress of mistresses, / O you, all my pleasures! o you, all my obligations! / You will remember the beauty of caresses, / The comfort of the hearth and the charm of the evenings / Mother of memories, mistress of mistresses!]

This first stanza exemplifies the general principle whereby a descriptive or declarative first-person utterance in the repeated (first and last) lines frames a second-person address to the beloved. A broad wave-like effect is created through the six stanzas, in which an initial exclamation by the solitary lover on his balcony sets up, each time, a dip into remembered intimacy, leading in turn to an emergence to the same exclamation – now itself ambiguously poised between reinforcement and recollection.

In Debussy's reading of this formalized play with time and intimacy, he keeps the vocal line the same for each of the repeated lines but subtly varies the texture or harmony of the pianistic backdrop. He further imparts his own formal rhythm to the whole through audible interrelationships between the opening vocal gestures of alternating stanzas. The low, declamatory style that recurs for the second and fourth stanzas in stark contrast to the sweeping soprano extravagances of the first and third, for example, sensitively highlights Baudelaire's long-range rhyme between 'Les soirs illuminés par l'ardeur du char*bon*' (evenings illuminated by the glow of the coal, stanza 2) and 'La nuit s'épaississait ainsi qu'une cloi*son*' (the night was thickening like a wall, stanza 4). The most musical flexibility, finally, is appropriately saved for Baudelaire's closing stanza, where the voice, too, is partly freed from its repetitions to capture the altered expressive force from first line – 'Ces serments, ces parfums' (those sermons, those perfumes) – to last: 'O serments! ô parfums!'

The other songs show comparable ingenuity. In the second, 'Harmonie du soir' (whose third line 'the sounds and perfumes turn in the evening air' would later provide the epigraph for one of Debussy's piano preludes), the poem's *pantoum* form – where the second and fourth lines of each four-line stanza become the first and third of the next – draws the reader directly into the 'languorous vertigo' it evokes. Debussy sets the many repeated lines with a fluctuation between near-exact recollection and unpredictable variation – thus enacting, in the evanescent sounds of his music, the imperfection of reminiscence that is the poem's main theme. In the delicately lyrical third song, 'Le Jet d'eau', the refrain that recurs between passionate stanzas to invoke a fountain – 'the spray of water that soothes its thousand flowers' – draws from Debussy a melody of simple, folk-like innocence. Having changed one word of the refrain – 'lueurs' (glimmers) becomes 'pâleurs' (palenesses) – he saves his most delicate harmonic shudder for this word's last appearance.[64] As for the two sonnets, finally, it is enough to single out the similar depth of response to a single word in 'Recueillement' (Contemplation), where, after the halting, fragmentary setting of the first line, the second – 'You called for the night; it descends; here it is' – settles onto a crystalline chord of arrival like a gift. A hint at the composer's symbolic motivations emerges when the same chord recurs, resonantly rescored, to launch the beautiful final image: 'And, like a long shroud trailing toward the east / Hear, my dear, hear the footsteps of the gentle night.'

It has been said that the Baudelaire songs stand somewhat outside the mainstream of Debussy's development, and there is no doubt that Verlaine's understated verse proved a more lasting resource in his consolidation of a song style oriented more towards 'declamation' than traditional 'singing'.[65] (A crucial step in this consolidation was to occur with his return to Verlaine in 1890–91 for the *Trois mélodies de Paul Verlaine* and the first volume of *Fêtes galantes*). But to recall Debussy's Baudelairean invocation to Vasnier of an ideal music 'supple enough, forceful enough, to adapt itself to the lyrical movements of the soul and the caprices of dreams', the prosodic suppleness and expressive force of his selections from *Les Fleurs du mal* offered him an ideal textual forum to test the limits of his lyrical powers as he grappled head-on with the overweening model of Wagner. Alongside the orchestral refinement of *La Damoiselle élue*, the formal ingenuity of his *Cinq Poèmes* invaluably tempered Debussy's readerly resources as he moved on to even richer acts of poetic appropriation.

A Pivotal Time

During the few years just before and after 1890 several new inspirations came into Debussy's life. All through the summer of 1889, the brand new Eiffel Tower – iron-strutted monument to industrial modernity – presided over the International Exhibition on the Champ de Mars. Debussy spent long afternoons with his old friends Bonheur and Dukas and a newer acquaintance, Robert Godet (a Swiss linguist who would become a lifelong correspondent), perusing the exotic musical entertainments clustered on the Left Bank of the Seine. In part, this was an opportunity to refresh his enthusiasm for Russian music, and add a first taste of Mussorgsky, at the orchestral concerts conducted by Nikolai Rimsky-Korsakov. But more startling revelations came from two

Far Eastern productions: the intricate percussion music of the Javanese *gamelan* – years later Debussy would recall the 'counterpoint that makes Palestrina look like child's play' – and the theatre troupe from Annam (now Vietnam) whose dramatic spectacle and piercingly expressive instrumentation inspired Debussy, according to Godet, to 'irreverent comparisons with Bayreuth'.[66]

Coming exactly at the time of his Baudelaire songs, these revelations of radically different musical conceptions may have played some role in Debussy's attainment, around this time, of a more manageable aesthetic distance from Wagner. A second trip to Bayreuth in August 1889 resulted in a letter to Guiraud sarcastically bemoaning the fact that Wagner had not 'supped with Pluto' after composing *Meistersinger* – that is, before finishing the 'tricky contraption' of *Der Ring des Nibelungen* – and woefully admitting a growing detachment even from his 'beloved *Tristan*'.[67] But Debussy was never to resolve his relationship to this particular precursor in any simple fashion. Soon after the second Bayreuth trip, Emmanuel jotted down some conversations between Debussy and Guiraud that clearly encapsulated his lasting ambivalence. On one hand, Debussy was eager to relegate Wagner to a 'classical' past:

> Wagner develops in the classical manner. In the place of the architectural themes of a symphony, occurring at specified points, he has themes representing things and people, but he develops these themes in a symphonic manner. He derives from Bach and Beethoven, as we see in *Tristan* and *Meistersinger* – to say nothing of his orchestra which is a development and enlargement of the classical orchestra.[68]

But on the other hand, he continually evokes *Tristan* as a model for musical themes that 'do no violence to the action' and even 'suggest the visual scene'.[69] This contradictory perspective on

Wagnerian 'themes' would persist right through to his polemical defences of his own opera over a decade later.

To his credit, Debussy was willing to acknowledge his own contradictions. As Emmanuel reports it, after his ringing calls for a music 'neither major nor minor' whose 'rhythms cannot be contained within bars' led him in turn to a series of portentous claims – 'there is no theory'; 'pleasure is the law'; 'music cannot be learnt' – Guiraud saw fit to remind him that he had, actually, spent ten years at the Conservatoire. 'I can't reconcile all this', Debussy frankly admitted, and acknowledged that he could only claim such freedom 'because I have been through the mill'.[70] In truth, by this point he had not quite emerged from the 'mill', for it was only in 1890 that he completed his fourth and final Prix de Rome *envoi*, a *Fantaisie* for piano and orchestra in which many have heard the most direct influence, in any of his works, of the Javanese *gamelan*.[71]

The *Fantaisie* was another work that long remained unperformed, for on learning that Vincent d'Indy, the conductor of the intended Société nationale premiere, was planning to cut two of the three movements for reasons of timing, Debussy withdrew the orchestral parts. His explanation, that he would prefer 'a sufficient performance of three movements over a satisfying one of the first alone', is understandable given that the work makes use of the 'cyclic' principle of unity d'Indy himself championed, on the model of César Franck, for French instrumental music.[72] (To put it simply, cyclic works feature a recurrence of the main thematic material from movement to movement.) But there may have been deeper reasons for the decision, for while the *Fantaisie* was to find a marginal place in the concerto repertoire after its posthumous premiere, the shallow influence of *gamelan* style arguably does little to enrich the problematic dramatic unfolding later characterized by Debussy in a letter to the younger composer Edgard Varèse as a 'slightly ridiculous struggle' between piano and orchestra.[73]

With Debussy's failure to submit the *Fantaisie* to the Institut and his refusal to write an overture for an official concert of his *envois*, his Conservatoire years dwindled to an anticlimactic close. Supporting himself in part by hack work writing piano arrangements of Saint-Saëns, Schumann and Wagner for the music publishers Durand, and in part by selling several minor piano pieces, he turned enthusiastically to the Bohemian nightlife of Paris's cafés, cabarets and taverns. An encounter with dramatist Gabriel Mourey at the Taverne Weber would lead to various abortive proposals for collaboration; at the Chat Noir, a nightclub famed for exotic entertainments, he met a more significant musical friend in the eccentric pianist and composer Erik Satie. Some have argued that Satie's iconoclastic music – forged in part on a cabaret piano, in part at the 'Salon de la Rose et Croix' of the Sâr Peladan, one of the *fin de siècle*'s many self-aggrandizing mystics – had a catalysing influence on Debussy's radical harmonic explorations; indeed Satie would later style himself 'The Precursor'. While the depth of this influence has arguably been overstated, it is clear from a dedicated copy of the *Cinq Poèmes de Charles Baudelaire* – 'For Erik Satie, graceful medieval musician, who has strayed into this century, for the joy of his beloved friend Claude-A Debussy' – that Debussy found much inspiration in this interaction with a more resolutely marginal model of avant-garde musical life, even as he struggled to find a place for his more refined radicalism within Paris's mainstream musical institutions.

The struggle was to be aided in unpredictable ways by the circulation of the *Cinq Poèmes de Charles Baudelaire* in musico-literary circles. In the first place, the arch-*wagnériste* poet, novelist and playwright Catulle Mendès was so struck by the experience of Debussy's '*musiques baudelairiennes*' at a private performance *chez* Chausson that he sought him out with an opera libretto cobbled together out of various sources including Corneille's *Le Cid*. The cultural prominence of Mendès, who had previously provided librettos for operas by Chabrier and Massenet (and later became a chronicler of literary Symbolism), may partly explain Debussy's agreement to begin work on the opera, *Rodrigue et Chimène*.[74] But his persistence with the project through nearly three years of exasperated labour is nonetheless somewhat baffling from a literary and musical perspective.

In his conversations with Guiraud not long before, Debussy had sketched a vision of his ideal librettist:

> One who only hints at what is to be said. The ideal would be two associated dreams. No place, nor time. No big scene. No compulsion on the musician, who must complete and give body to the work of the poet . . . A painting executed in grey is the ideal. No developments merely for the sake of developments . . . No discussion or arguments between the characters whom I see at the mercy of life or destiny.[75]

Eerily prophetic of the Maeterlinck play Debussy would eventually set in *Pelléas et Mélisande,* this description could not be further removed from the Mendès libretto Dukas described as a 'motley assortment of Parnassian bric-à-brac and Spanish barbarism'.[76] In fact, Mendès had once propounded, in an 1876 article on ways to avoid slavish Wagnerian imitation, a few general points about operatic aesthetics – for example the need to draw 'poetry and music into intimate union' and to break 'the framework of the old symmetrical melody' – vaguely in line with Debussyan ideals. But beyond such superficial overlap the true aesthetic distance between the two is clear, for example, from Mendès's description of the modern orchestra as a 'great vat, in which all the molten elements of the drama may be heard seething together' – and indeed his emphasis on a 'lofty heroic action' and a 'great final emotion'.[77]

It is impossible to judge Debussy's instrumental conception of *Rodrigue et Chimène* against Mendès's 'great vat', for he had not yet orchestrated his draft of three acts when he abandoned the opera some time in 1893. Regarding his handling of action and emotion, on the other hand, it is clear from the performing version by musicologist Richard Langham Smith and composer Edison Denisov (premiered in 1993 by the Opéra de Lyon) that Debussy's lengthy period of work on 'this Opera, in which everything is against me' was not without value.[78] Seen as a kind of personal 'test opera' that reached reasonably complete dramatic shape, at least, before Debussy put it aside in favour of a more congenial libretto, there is actually plenty in *Rodrigue* to admire. Apart from certain *longueurs* (not all solely attributable to Mendès) the pacing within and between scenes is generally deft; the range of affect is broad, extending from delicately hieratic choral writing reminiscent of *La Damoiselle élue* through to a boisterous drinking song and a blazingly bombastic crowd scene.

One particularly effective portrayal of 'the thousand sensations of a character' – to recall Debussy's vision for *Diane au bois* – occurs at the pivotal moment of Act II when the hero Rodrigue, summoned to revenge an insult to his father Don Diègue by Don Gomez, father of his beloved Chimènes, is plunged into tortured indecision over the conflicting pressures of duty and love. Mendès could hardly have marked out the conflict more broadly. But even so, Debussy's sensitive pacing, for example in the delicately poised silence after 'The father of . . .' and the soft vocal blossoming on 'Chimène' when Rodrigue finally utters the name several dramatic phrases later, helps unearth as much 'character' as could be found in the hackneyed language. Later, he also manages to impart considerable nobility to the dying breaths of Don Gomez, dramatically offsetting the unaccompanied cry when Chimènes realizes that she is bound by custom to seek her lover's death in return.

Such evidence of dramatic care aside, the possibility that Debussy set some store by his labours on *Rodrigue et Chimène* is borne out by his dedication of the draft score to a significant new figure in his life. 'To Mademoiselle Gabrielle Dupont' reads the dedication on the first act, dated April 1890. A green-eyed milliner from Normandy described by Debussy's friend René Peter as 'the least frivolous blonde he ever met', Gabrielle, or Gaby, who met him early in 1890, soon became involved in a romantic partnership that would last almost to the end of the century.[79] No doubt their relationship was a key stimulus for Debussy's decision, finally, to leave the family home. In June 1891, he and Gaby moved together into a sparsely furnished apartment at 42 rue de Londres.

Flimsy recompense as it might seem, the dedication of *Rodrigue* can thus be read as an initial sign of the gratitude Debussy would eventually owe Gaby for her stoic support during the years in which, from the shakiest of material circumstances, he produced the compositional readings that secured his place in music history. The first of these arose, again, from the impact of the Baudelaire songs. During a meeting at a café, the symbolist poet A.-Ferdinand Hérold told Debussy he had shown the songs to another writer closely connected to French *wagnériste* circles. Apparently Stéphane Mallarmé – who had composed a profound homage to Baudelaire in his prose 'Literary Symphony' as long ago as 1865 – was so struck by the musical ambition in these settings from *Les Fleurs du mal* that he implored Hérold to ask Debussy to collaborate on a musico-dramatic presentation of his own famous Eclogue, *L'après-midi d'un faune*.[80] Although this production was never to take the stage, the opportunity to work closely with the most exacting literary thinker of his day was to prove of crucial significance in Debussy's ongoing search for a music that 'clothes the poetry, to convey the sensation of something truly lived'.

2

A Dream from Which One Draws Back the Veils

An effusive letter of February 1893 from Debussy to the wealthy businessman and fellow Mallarméan André Poniatowski captures the combination of professional insecurity and aesthetic intransigence with which he entered into his thirties. On the material side of things, he complained of the 'war of pinpricks' he was suffering from his family, who found him 'a much too unproductive son, at least as concerns glory'. But even as he acknowledged that the 'castles in Spain that had been built on the anticipation of my future glory have sadly collapsed into the water', he gazed out on the more successful musical productions of the season with a jaundiced eye.[1]

Established figures and newer arrivals were equally subject to scorn. The premiere of Massenet's opera *Werther*, based on Goethe's novel, inspired a harangue against the misappropriation of great literature:

> [It exemplifies] that deplorable habit that consists in taking something that has its own high quality, and mistranslating its spirit into facile, amiable sentimentalities; it is the same old story of Faust butchered by Gounod, or Hamlet unluckily deranged by M. Ambroise Thomas. Truly one condemns such people who fabricate false bank notes out of the work of their betters.

To this premonitory hint at the respect with which he himself would approach the work of his literary 'betters' Mallarmé and Maeterlinck, Debussy added a prudish sniff at recent 'realistic' musical trends. 'What you cannot imagine', he wrote about the 'symphony-drama' *La Vie du Poète* by a close contemporary Gustave Charpentier, 'is the lack of taste shown by the work. To give a little example, the last movement of the symphony represents the Moulin-Rouge, where the Poet (hard to believe, I know) has washed up in failure; there is even a prostitute uttering orgasmic cries!' In the face of such shallow literalism, and of the 'snobs' who 'in fear of passing for cretins' hailed Charpentier's work as a masterpiece, Debussy hurled a characteristic outburst: 'Music! It is a dream from which one draws back the veils! It is not the expression of a sentiment, it is the sentiment itself!'

It is not always easy to imagine from such assertions what would have qualified as music that attained to Debussy's dream. Here, while excoriating Charpentier for 'dragging music through the mud', he raised the familiar foil of Palestrina, in whose music 'the emotion is not translated (as it has come to be since) by cries, but by melodic arabesques – in other words, we might say, by the actual contour'. The ensuing decade was to see the completion of several works that, in their deployment of flexible melodic contour, would come to define the Debussyan 'arabesque'. In the shorter term, the letter to Poniatowski ended by prematurely announcing the completion of a string quartet and a set of songs. The quartet was to become a central work in the repertoire. The songs, ironically, proved less successful.

The irony springs from the fact that the texts for the *Proses lyriques* were written by Debussy himself. This Wagnerian adoption of a double role might have been expected to deliver a strong exemplification of the strict standards he was applying to others. But while the texts were deemed at the time of enough merit to be published in a journal edited by the poets Francis Vielé-Griffin and

Henri de Régnier, they read now as the predictable pastiches of a secondary literary *métier*.[2] Alongside their Baudelairean sensuality, Verlainian delicacy and Rossettian mysticism, the most striking addition to Debussy's poetic palette in the *Proses lyriques* is the glimpse, in the last, of a more up-to-date, realistic sense of modern urban recreation:

> Sunday, the stations are crazy!
> Everyone is under way
> For the suburbs of adventure,
> Saying goodbye to each other
> With bewildered gestures!
> Sunday the trains run quickly,
> Devoured by insatiable tunnels;
> And the good signals on the roads
> Exchange with a single eye,
> Mechanical impressions.

The kinship between this vision of Sunday departures and the famous depiction of the 'suburbs of adventure' in Seurat's 1886 canvas *A Sunday Afternoon on the Island of Grande Jatte* suggests some sensitivity, on Debussy's part, to contemporary social concerns.[3] But musically, several moments in these songs bring to mind his own strictures about expression. In the closing lines of the first ('Of Dream'), for example, a restrained setting of the nod to *Parsifal* ('The knights have died / On the road to the Grail!') prepares a bizarre image ('Hands so mad, so frail, / In the days when swords sang for them!') expressed through overwrought climactic leaps. Similar bathetic excess emerges for the imprecation 'Come! Come! Hands of salvation!/ To break the panes of falsehood, / To break the panes of wickedness' late in the fourth song ('Of flowers'). To put it ungenerously, the *Proses lyriques* can be said to illustrate the degree to which Debussy was dependent upon verbal material crafted by his literary betters as a stimulus to effective compositional readings.

At this point, indeed, his work on the most challenging of all such material, Mallarmé's long poem *L'après-midi d'un faune*, was well under way. According to Poniatowski, 'long discussions' between poet and composer had begun as early as 1890.[4] But the fruit of these discussions had yet to find its final form. When the vocal score of *La Damoiselle élue* was first published in 1893 it included an announcement of a forthcoming multipart work: 'In preparation, *Prelude, Interludes, and Final Paraphrase for L'après-midi d'un faune*'.

A Concert, a Play and a New Friendship

While the *Prélude* Debussy eventually distilled from this elaborate vision would not be heard for many months, *La Damoiselle élue* belatedly received its premiere at the Société nationale on 8 April 1893. The warm response of Vincent d'Indy, director of the Société, was to prove of great practical value. Amidst the mixed responses of the critics, at least one – Charles Darcours, in *Le Figaro* – was able to celebrate this 'sensual, decadent, even somewhat over-ripe' work as a valuable infusion of new blood to the venerable society.[5] But the most immediate benefit of the concert was a more private one. The close contact between Debussy and Ernest Chausson, whose *Poème de l'amour et la mer* appeared on the same programme, led to a significant deepening of their friendship. Over somewhat more than a year, dozens of letters would testify to the importance of a relationship which, though never attaining the intimacy of a *tutoiement*, was to prove a crucial support during difficult times.

In the weeks following the *Damoiselle* premiere Debussy, who had not yet abandoned *Rodrigue et Chimène*, took part in another of Mendès's *wagnériste* projects. A series of public lectures on *Das*

Rheingold and *Die Walküre* featured musical examples played on two pianos by Debussy and Raul Pugno, a one-time prodigy who was then reviving his virtuoso piano career. Although widely seen as a great success this venture only deepened Debussy's disillusionment with his librettist's inveterate self-aggrandizement. In a wry note to Chausson about Mendès's tendency to glorify Wagner's poetry over his music, Debussy suggested that it all seemed a roundabout way of saying that 'if he, Mendès, had not made any music, that was because one could do quite well without it'.[6]

Happily, just as his exasperation with Mendès was becoming terminal, Debussy first encountered a play that seemed the perfect embodiment of the dramatic ideals he had envisioned in discussion with Guiraud. He had, in fact, previously sought unsuccessfully to use a play by Maurice Maeterlinck, *La Princesse Maleine*, as an opera libretto. Now, in 1893, his attendance at the first Parisian production of the same author's *Pelléas et Mélisande* – whose printed text he had already possessed for some months – was to inspire new musico-dramatic ideas that would prove pivotal for his own career and for the history of modern opera. Strangely, Debussy made no mention of this experience when writing to Chausson of his entrapment in 'banal occupations'.[7] But the closer contact with Chausson was immediately to bring with it a musical discovery of great significance for his consolidation of his operatic aesthetic.

In a letter of 24 May that anticipated Debussy's pending visit to Chausson's country estate at Luzancy, Chausson noted that 'the new Mussorgsky works will probably be here.'[8] There has been some debate about the history of Debussy's encounters with Mussorgsky's music (for one thing, he later insisted to the critic Pierre Lalo that this name had never been invoked during his youthful travels in Russia).[9] But it is clear that a significant new phase in his appreciation for a composer who was, over time, to displace Wagner in his musical pantheon was reached during lengthy evenings spent playing through Mussorgsky's opera *Boris*

Ernest Chausson and his wife Jeanne. The well-off older composer was an important supporter for a brief period in the early 1890s.

Godunov during two short stays in the country with Chausson, Bonheur and Chausson's brother-in-law Henri Lerolle (another important supporter) in the early summer of 1893.

Soon after his return from this 'suburban adventure' Debussy and Gaby moved to a new apartment at 10 rue Gustave-Doré, in the north-west corner of Paris, where they would remain throughout the remaining years of their liaison. A fortnight later he learned that his attempt, through Henri de Régnier, to secure Maeterlinck's permission for an opera on *Pelléas et Mélisande* had been successful. After playing through the incomplete *Rodrigue* one last time for Dukas, who appreciated the dramatic breadth of some scenes but found the libretto vapid, he finally put Mendès aside in favour of Maeterlinck.[10] Chausson, caught in endless toils on his own opera *Le Roi Arthus*, could only respond with envy at the early progress reports: 'One scene of *Pelléas* completed! And the fourth *Prose*

Debussy at the piano during an 1893 summer visit to the Chausson estate at Luzancy. One crucial discovery was Mussorgsky's opera *Boris Godunov*.

lyrique! How quickly you are proceeding!'[11] But Debussy was soon confessing that his struggles to shake off the Wagnerian yoke were not yet over. 'The ghost of old Klingsor alias R. Wagner appeared in one bar', he wrote in early October, 'and I had to tear it all up and begin again, in search of a delicate chemistry of more personal phrases. Forcing myself to become just as much Pelléas et Mélisande, I have been searching for music behind all the veils it gathers around itself, even for its most ardent devotees.'[12]

Musical Societies, Esoteric and Otherwise

The recurrence, here, of the image previously invoked to Poniatowski – 'Music! It is a dream from which one draws back the veils!' – underlines the recalcitrance with which Debussy clung to idealistic visions even in the most precarious circumstances. At times, his idealism shaded into elitist disdain. Reporting on some of de Régnier's musings about the way certain French words had become tarnished through over-use, for example, Debussy suggested to Chausson that a similar case could be made for certain 'banalized' musical harmonies. In this light, he insisted:

> Truly music should have been a hermetic science, guarded by texts requiring such long and difficult interpretation that it would surely have discouraged the mob of people that treat it with the same thoughtlessness they use when reaching for a pocket handkerchief! . . . Instead of searching to open up Art to the public, I propose the foundation of a 'Society of Musical Esotericism'.[13]

While it may be possible to discern some characteristic irony here, it is harder to salvage the distasteful overtones that emerge later when, calling for a 'school of Neomusicians' devoted to the integrity of 'the admirable symbols of music', Debussy blames the degradation of taste he saw all around on 'the motto inscribed on all our monuments: Liberty, Equality, Fraternity – wonderful words, fit for cab drivers at best!'[14]

It would be simplistic to read such rhetoric as a clue to strong anti-Republican beliefs. A growing cultural nationalism aside, Debussy's political inclinations never received coherent formulation. His vision of a 'Society for Musical Esotericism' is better read as a telling emanation from a pivotal moment in the evolution of European art music, during which the tradition of broadly accessible expression that had culminated in the intoxications of late-nineteenth-century *wagnérisme* was giving way to a newly problematic relationship between avant-garde composers and the concert-going public. Chausson, who was quick to dismiss Debussy's self-doubts with an assertion that 'your music is of an essentially modern, and refined, sensibility', may be credited for sensing some of the refinement with which Debussy would capture, in the series of major works that first took shape around 1893, an exemplary modern tension between esoteric and popular musical ideals.[15]

Even as Debussy's correspondence with Chausson entered its most involved phase, he began a second friendship that was to prove just as significant during the evolution of these works. Pierre Louÿs, a somewhat younger writer, had also been an habitué of the Bailly bookstore and Mallarmé's Tuesday evening soirées (the so-called *mardis*). In late 1893 his friendship with Debussy also took on new warmth, and progressed rapidly to the *tutoiement* never shared with Chausson. In early November, Debussy and Louÿs travelled together to Brussels to visit the esteemed violinist Eugène Ysaÿe, who was soon to premiere Debussy's string quartet; then to Ghent, for a meeting with Maeterlinck. Louÿs gave conflicting reports of the latter 'marvellous' encounter, claiming at one point that the timidity of composer and playwright alike had effectively made him the spokesman for both.[16] But while Debussy also noted Maeterlinck's skittishness in his account to Chausson, he went on praise his surprisingly helpful suggestions about possible cuts to the play.[17]

Back in Paris, work proceeded both on the new opera and the string quartet, for which Debussy had recently secured a publishing contract. He played and sang the first completed scenes of *Pelléas et Mélisande* for Lerolle and Bonheur, but not for Dukas, whose exacting opinion he wished to save for a more advanced stage. After much strenuous revision, the string quartet was premiered by the Ysaÿe quartet at the Société nationale on 29 December 1893, alongside works by Franck and d'Indy. In the critical response, guarded appreciation mixed with bafflement at Debussy's 'ingenuity', 'subtlety' and 'delicacy of thought'.[18] In other words, this exuberantly inventive and colourful work was initially received as an embodiment of the esotericism Debussy had hailed in his letter to Chausson. Chausson himself, who was to have been the dedicatee, seems from Debussy's pained response to have shared that reaction. Dedicating the work instead to the Ysaÿe quartet, Debussy promised to write him a 'nobler' replacement.[19] But he would not return to significant chamber music composition for over two decades.

In the ensuing months Debussy circulated through musical milieux that differed, to varying degrees, from his ideal 'Society for Musical Esotericism'. The aesthetic profile of the factional Société nationale, first of all, is best described as somewhat contradictory. Chausson admitted to Debussy that his own compositional shortcomings could be blamed in part on 'the aesthetic of the Société', whose concerts 'resemble, at times, a sort of doctoral examination' – but affirmed nonetheless that it was, all the same, 'the place in Paris where one hears the best modern music'.[20] Debussy, while developing his ambivalent relationship to the Société, confronted a different flavour of exclusivity at the 'Wagnerian séances' hosted by Chausson's mother-in-law Mme Escudier in her elegant apartment near the Parc Monceau, where he played several music dramas at the piano, and at the fashionable soirées of various society hostesses, where he presented his own music.

In spite of his previous high society experience with Mme von Meck, it was with a mixture of bemusement and disgust that Debussy now wrote to Chausson:

> I hardly recognize myself! *I am now to be seen in the salons,* making appropriate smiles, or imagine, I am directing choruses at the house of the countess Zamoiska! (yes sir!) . . . there is also Mme de St. Marceaux who has decided that I am a talent of the

first order! It is all to die laughing! But truly one would have to be terribly weak of soul to allow oneself to become stuck in this kind of glue![21]

Still, while he would never become a true *salon* habitué like Marcel Proust or Gabriel Fauré it is clear that Debussy's soul was not quite strong enough to resist the pressures such exalted company exerted towards the appearance, at least, of moral respectability. On 17 February 1894, he accompanied a singer who had also worked with Chausson, Thérèse Roger, in the premiere of two of his *Proses lyriques*. Barely a week later, in letters written in haste to Lerolle and to the Société composer Pierre de Bréville as Debussy prepared to depart for a second trip to Brussels, he blithely announced his engagement to Thérèse.[22]

Clearly, this impetuous decision can be attributed to Debussy's wish to attain, at a step, a degree of bourgeois respectability. The wide astonishment it elicited would not be faced until after this second Belgian sojourn. This time, Debussy travelled to Brussels to participate in the first full-length concert devoted to his music. On one of four programmes presented under the auspices of the *Salon de la Libre Esthétique* (Salon of the Free Aesthetic), the latest instantiation of an annual art exhibition organized by the impresario Octave Maus, Ysaÿe led a performance of the string quartet and conducted an ensemble of musicians from the Brussels Conservatoire in *La Damoiselle élue*. Thérèse Roger, summoned in haste when the contracted soprano fell ill, sang in the cantata and again joined Debussy in two of the *Proses lyriques*.

The other three concerts, which presented works by Chausson, Franck and d'Indy alongside works by Beethoven and Schubert, can be seen as a particularly blatant illustration of the claim by the modern French school to be the heirs of the 'Great Tradition' of Viennese classicism.[23] Such a context vividly frames the ironic tones with which Debussy, through his quartet's sophisticated dialogues

with traditional models, had engaged with the same heritage. In his case, the refractory take on the past in the sole work he dignified with an opus number, 'opus 10', was further compounded by its subtle negotiation, through an intricate post-Beethovenian harmonic 'argument', with the syntactical implications of *wagnérisme*.[24]

In retrospect, it is possible to see amidst the myriad artistic tendencies on display at the same salon – from Impressionism and Pre-Raphaelism through all the various flavours of post-Impressionism – at least a few whose negotiations amidst the vestiges of tradition and the new promises of modernist system suggestively parallel the central concerns of Debussy's quartet. One critic, the *wagnériste* Maurice Kufférath, who heard the work as a kind of musical 'pointillism' akin to certain 'neo-Japoniste' painters of Montmartre, fortuitously stumbled on the 'systematic' elements and exotic influences that can, with careful consideration, best indicate the most fruitful of such parallels, and thus further qualify lazy generalizations about Debussy's Impressionism.[25] At the same time, it is worth noting the emphasis in the salon's lectures and exhibits alike on an erosion of the boundary between 'art' and 'craft' – in other words, on a more inclusive vision of modern aesthetics than the 'esotericist' ideals Debussy had been propounding to Chausson.[26]

However professionally significant and aesthetically suggestive the Brussels 'Debussy festival' may have been, it was overshadowed on his return to Paris by the aftershocks of his announced engagement. A first letter to Chausson, hailing the 'path full of light' that promised to lead him out of 'shady places', affirmed a determination to 'carry a completely new soul into a new life' and ended (after a request for money) with gratitude for the charming things Mme Chausson had written to Thérèse.[27] But such sentiments proved short-lived. Within days, Chausson was asking Debussy to explain certain inconvenient facts (he was still living with Gaby) as well as mysterious revelations about moral depravities in his past. His explanations were received as lies; the engagement was broken off; the friendship between the two composers came to an end.

The Wagnerian evenings *chez* Mme Escudier having also been cut short, it was left to Louÿs to mollify the equally scandalized Mme de Sainte-Marceaux. Urbanely arguing that 'a young man cannot just dismiss, like a chamber-maid, a mistress who has lived with him for two years', he went on to insist that 'as for the noises that have been reported about his previous life, I stand guarantor that those are monstrous calumnies'.[28] It seems from his letters to others that Louÿs was not quite as convinced about Debussy's blamelessness as he claimed. But whatever truth there may have been behind the calumnies, neither he nor Lerolle was ready, like Chausson, to end their relations with Debussy. Indeed, from this point the friendship with Louÿs entered its most intimate phase.

A Mallarméan Musical Allegory

It is, in truth, profoundly ironic that Louÿs presumed to stand as moral guarantor for anyone. A few months later he would be sending Debussy the first reports of the exotic adventures that would render him, over the next few years, a typical 'sex tourist'. Inspired by his friend and fellow-writer André Gide, the first such adventure deflected him from a third Bayreuth pilgrimage to the famed oasis town of Biskra in Algeria. In late July he crowed to Debussy of his dalliance there with 'a young person of sixteen years who has the most depraved morals and a name like a little bird: Meryem bent-Ali'.[29] By the next year he was taking perverse pleasure in reporting the young age of various sexual companions in Spain. Eventually, announcing a return to Paris from Algeria with a more mature 'colonial product', Zohra ben-Brahim, in tow as a mistress, he celebrated this latest liaison in terms that recall the fetishization

The writer Pierre Louÿs in Constantinople, during one of the sybaritic tours that nourished his literary exoticism.

of exotic flesh in countless contemporary paintings: 'how pretty it is, on white sheets, the body of a woman in chocolate'.[30]

According to another young writer friend, the dramatist René Peter, Debussy disdained Louÿs's sexual experimentation as 'useless monkey-business'.[31] At any rate, he was content to 'work like a tram-horse' throughout the summer of 1894 'in the sole company of Pelléas and Mélisande'.[32] Soon, finding that these two characters were 'refusing to descend from their tapestry', he expanded his labours to other projects. In one of these he proposed to Ysaÿe 'three *Nocturnes* for principal violin and orchestra' which would, by deploying the orchestra in separate groups, present 'a study in the diverse arrangements that can be given through a single colour, as for example in painting, a study in Gray'.[33] This inchoate vision later gave rise to a tenacious association between Debussy's *Trois Nocturnes* and the painted 'Nocturnes' of James MacNeill Whistler (which bear such subtitles as 'Symphony in Blue and Gold'), in spite of the fact that this work would evolve radically over the five years it took to complete. (Years later Debussy pointedly scorned the journalistic conceit that labelled him 'the Whistler of music'.[34]) More tangible progress can be deduced from the publication contract Debussy signed in October for the *Prélude à l'après-midi d'un faune*. The significance of this contract was to extend beyond its immediate recompense of 200 francs, for the publisher, Georges Hartmann, was subsequently to sustain Debussy with a regular stipend while honouring many urgent

Debussy relaxing in Pierre Louÿs's apartment with Zohra bent-Brahim, the writer's Algerian mistress.

requests for extra money – and tolerating endless delays in the provision of promised scores.

On 22 December 1894 the *Prélude à l'après-midi d'un faune* finally received its premiere at the Société nationale. The Swiss conductor Gustave Doret, who later recalled the rare sensation behind his back of an audience 'completely subjugated', rewarded the enthusiastic final applause with an immediate repetition.[35] By Doret's account, the orchestral musicians had been equally captivated all through the meticulous rehearsals in Debussy's presence. Critical response, on the other hand, was less generous. For one surprising example, Charles Darcours – who had previously hailed the composer's literary sensibility in *La Damoiselle élue* – now recoiled, as if facing one stage of refinement too far. 'Such pieces are amusing to write,' he sniffed, 'but not at all to listen to.'[36]

Perhaps his annoyance can be explained by reference to the greater difficulty of the text that had inspired this new work. No doubt the problem was compounded by the fact that Debussy's reading of Mallarmé (unlike all his previous text-settings) unfolded in wordless orchestral sound. And over time, his evasiveness in response to the obvious question about his prelude's relationship to the poem *L'après-midi d'un faune* ended up enshrining a received wisdom even more deleterious to the understanding of his skills as a reader than the association of the *Nocturnes* with Whistler. The principal point of reference would be the flippant reply he gave to a query from the prominent critic Henri Gauthier-Villars:

> The *prélude à l'après-midi d'un Faune* ! . . . Is it perhaps that which remains of the dream at the tip of the faun's flute? More precisely, it is the general impression of the Poem, because in trying to follow it more closely, the music would run out of breath like a dray horse competing for the grand Prix with a thoroughbred.[37]

Although he proceeded to scatter a few gnomic hints about closer affinities, the offhand comment about a 'general impression' has had more lasting impact. Indeed a consensus eventually emerged that the change of title from 'prelude, interludes and final paraphrase' to 'prelude' signalled an abandonment of direct paraphrase in favour of a vague, prefatory gloss on the poem's overall mood or tone.

The immediate responses of Debussy's confidants support a different conclusion. Louÿs wrote in enthusiastic haste after the premiere: 'Your prelude is admirable. I wanted to tell you immediately on return. It was not possible to make a more delicious paraphrase of the verses both of us so loved.'[38] Mallarmé, having been invited by Debussy to hear 'the arabesques a possibly culpable pride has allowed me to believe were dictated by the Flute of your Faun', deemed the musical 'illustration' of his Eclogue 'a marvel! . . . which presents no dissonance with my text, if it is not in going further, truly, into nostalgia and light, with finesse, with malaise, with richness!'[39] Debussy echoed Mallarmé's description of the work as an 'illustration' when he congratulated another critic for being 'one of the very few to "understand" my modest attempt to illustrate this poem with concordant arabesques'.[40]

There are various reasons why it nonetheless became common to downplay the degree to which the *Prélude* might be said to paraphrase or illustrate Mallarmé's verses. For one thing, the contorted syntax that has rendered Mallarmé's oeuvre iconic of Symbolist mystery has also given rise to a presumption that it would be naive to try to unearth *any* clear thematic armature as the basis for musical paraphrase. On the other hand, while the *Prélude* has long held similarly iconic status – eminent post-war composer Pierre Boulez famously asserted that 'modern music awakens in the afternoon of a faun' – most analyses have exemplified a professional bias towards abstract, formalist explication, within which any reference to a lustful faun pursuing nymphs amidst lush pastoral settings can only seem an embarrassing irrelevance.[41]

For a finer appreciation of the *Prélude à l'après-midi d'un faune* as a musical reading, it helps to consider this reminiscence from his friend René Peter:

> In poetry, one never saw [Debussy] lapsing into mechanical citations, and undoubtedly he was prevented from doing so by the care he took, above all, to penetrate the general rhythm of a work and the idea that dominated it. From this sprang his devotion to Mallarmé, whose so-called obscurities appeared luminous to him because they superimposed themselves in combination over his own thought. He clearly never perceived in *L'après-midi d'un faune*, for example, each verse in separation like one of the branches that makes up a tree: he saw the entire forest with its millions of twigs, its glimpses of sunshine and its entwinings of gold and blue.[42]

In other words, the much-noted fact that Debussy responded to a poem of 110 lines with a piece exactly 110 bars long should not be read as the mark of a line-by-line 'paraphrase', but rather of a more embracing overview of the poem in its structured totality. This synthetic overview, in turn, became the basis of an elastic translation of the poem's 'general rhythm' into a musical form that rephrases in its own terms the 'idea' Mallarmé pursued through the words of his mythical protagonist, the faun.

The most important of the many ideas enfolded in the text is symbolized by the faun himself, a quasi-dramatic character whose divided body, half man and half goat, distils the duality between sensuous and intellectual experience.[43] This duality, projected through a web of cognates – mind and body; distanced vision and intimate touch; the palpable pleasures of speech and the austere symbols of writing – informs the text on multiple levels. It is given clearest definition within the 'general rhythm' as a contrast between two nymphs: one chaste and virginal; the other more sensuous and carnal. As Mallarmé's rhyming couplets gather expressive force along with the faun's pursuit of this paired object of desire, the notional separation gradually collapses, to set up a crux in which the duality between sense and sensation is enacted as an irresolvable conflict native to passionate lyrical utterance:

Je t'adore, courroux des vierges, ô délice
Farouche du sacré fardeau nu, qui se glisse
Pour fuir ma lèvre en feu buvant, comme un éclair
Tressaille! la frayeur secrète de la chair:
Des pieds de l'inhumaine au coeur de la timide
Que délaisse à la fois une innocence humide
De larmes folles ou de moins tristes vapeurs.

[I adore you, wrath of virgins, oh fierce / Delight of the sacred naked burden, which slides / To flee my lip drinking fire, like a lightning-bolt / Thrills! the secret terror of the flesh: / From the foot of the inhuman one to the heart of the shy, / Let all at once relinquish an innocence, humid / With mad tears or with less mournful vapours.]

This passage, whose palpable turn at '*Tressaille!*' (thrills!) from a hissing chain of sibilants to a more measured, liquid murmur exemplifies Mallarmé's most compelling verbal music, also carries darker undercurrents – 'wrath'; 'burden'; 'terror' – that trouble even the most energetic attempts to speak the role of the faun. When reading back to understand these darker hints, reader-performers will find themselves experiencing the same division, between eyes and mouth, mind and body . . .

In short, Mallarmé had crafted *L'après-midi d'un faune* (over years of revision) into an invitation to enact an agonistic confrontation with the lost ideals of vocal expression that preoccupied him all his life, even as he evolved into a pivotal figure for modern theories of

Stéphane Mallarmé at his writing desk in 1898, the year of his death.

'pure' or 'impersonal' poetry. Debussy's paraphrase, in turn, can be recognized from Peter's embracing perspective as an equivalent confrontation with fading expressive ideals.[44] At the simplest level of the musical illustration, for each of the contrasts between chaste and carnal nymphs Debussy wrote a contrast between solo wind instruments and the whole violin section. Simple as it may seem, this translation of Mallarmé's central idea actually offers a knowing reading of Romantic orchestral tradition. The most influential of all orchestration treatises – written by Hector Berlioz in the early 1840s – discusses all wind sounds in literary, culturally mediated tones, while singling out the violins as the most sensuous and 'penetrating' voice of the orchestra, 'at once passionate and chaste'.[45]

If this congruence with Mallarmé's formal rhythm can be made audible to any listener, full appreciation of the musical paraphrase also demands consideration of a second level of response. Debussy secreted within each of his main sonorous contrasts a sly reference to the recurring musical motives of Wagner's music dramas (the so-called 'leitmotifs'), keyed to Mallarmé's poem through the verbal labels that had become a central tool of Wagnerian exegesis (e.g., the 'Desire' and 'Solitude' leitmotifs in *Tristan und Isolde*).[46] This esoteric undercurrent persists even through the lyrical effusion – reminiscent of Tchaikovksy or Balakirev – sung by all strings together at the piece's heart. The result, as has been suggested about a similar procedure in *Pelléas et Mélisande*, is 'a sort of game' that is 'meant to be discovered'.[47] In other words, in the contrast between the audible pleasures of his orchestration and the harmonic references accessible only to those 'in the know', Debussy found a sophisticated way to paraphrase Mallarmé's enactment of a division (speech and writing) within the reader's experience of his poem.

The *Prélude à l'après-midi d'un faune* stands as the culmination of Debussy's early development as a musical reader. His ability to 'make an abstraction of the text' had become refined enough to facilitate, with Mallarmé's assistance, an allegorical reflection through musical form on the problematic relationship between listening and 'understanding' (to adopt his own scare quotes). At the same time, the pressing need in Symbolist circles to renew

One of Édouard Manet's illustrations for the first, 1876 edition of Mallarmé's *L'après-midi d'un faune*. The faun's features recall those of the poet himself.

over-used materials – recall de Régnier on 'tarnished' words – found programmatic realization through this studied treatment of the sound of sensuously singing violins, previously the default sound of Romantic orchestral lyricism. This seductive archetype of lyrical expression, now framed nostalgically within a soundscape dominated by pastoral winds, found fleeting new freshness even as it took its place alongside Mallarmé's lyric address (*'Je t'adore'*) as an artifice on the verge of fading away in favour of cooler, more impersonal artistic ideals.

The Bilitis Triptych: Sensuality as Allegory

Even in paraphrasing complex poetry with enough sophistication to satisfy the technocratic Boulez, Debussy maintained a sonorous surface beautiful enough to secure the *Prélude* pride of place, decades later, on CDs marketed (for example) as 'Debussy for Daydreaming'.[48] This basic contradiction marks his success at holding in solution – or in pastoral 'suspension' – the central dilemmas of his period at the threshold of modern music.[49] But the fact that the work's multi-levelled sophistication largely went unrecognized confirms the degree to which its Mallarméan refinement was already at odds with most of his audience. Indeed, whatever its mythic status in music history, the premiere of the *Prélude* in late 1894 – which received minimal notice in the press – hardly marked a breakthrough in Debussy's career.

Although he announced the completion, 'as of August 17, 1895', of the opera that would eventually occasion such a breakthrough, he still had years to wait for the epochal 1902 staging of *Pelléas et Mélisande*.[50] These intervening years, thinner in significant accomplishment than those just before, were partly consumed by abortive collaborations with Louÿs. An exchange about an opera on Cinderella (*Cendrelune*) persisted into 1898, even though Louÿs became so exasperated at one point that he told Debussy to write the libretto himself. A proposal for a ballet on Longus's early Greek romance *Daphnis and Chloe* foundered more quickly. A passing suggestion for another based on Louÿs's own novel *Aphrodite* – serially published in late 1895 to great acclaim – also led nowhere. Of all such proposals, Debussy took most enthusiastically to *La Saulaie*, a cantata on Louÿs's translation of another poem by Rossetti (*Willow Wood*), drafting several pages before abandoning it in 1900.[51]

There is wide agreement that the failure of all these collaborations betrays an essential difference of aesthetics. As his friend André Gide once put it, it is a mistake to associate Louÿs with the 'modern school', because he was actually 'as little modern as possible (I exaggerate a little), not Symbolist at all, but still of the preceding school of the Parnassians, of Gautier, Banville, Hugo, Hérédia'.[52] Furthermore, while Debussy was able to praise Louÿs's writing – at times with reservations, as Louÿs noted: 'I will always love your music more than you love my literature' – disagreement occasionally arose over musical issues.[53] Most notably, the letters of mid-1896 bear traces of a heated dispute about Louÿs's unqualified adulation for Wagner as 'the greatest man that has ever existed'.[54]

The possibility that Louÿs, belated Parnassian and unreconstructed *wagnériste*, ultimately remained 'out of step' with Debussy's evolving modernist sensibility should be borne in mind when considering the one significant work that did emerge from a confluence of their two arts. In late 1894 Louÿs published a book inspired by his experiences with Meryem bent-Ali: the *Songs of Bilitis, translated from the Greek for the first time by P.L.* A preface identified these hundred-odd prose poems as the recently discovered work of an unknown poetess from the sixth century BCE. In truth, they were by Louÿs himself. Given the book's *faux*-antiquarian concoction of erotic-exotic clichés – eager pubescent virgins; stolen embraces under Mediterranean skies; long-ago lesbian love affairs – it is easy enough to understand its immediate, continent-wide success.[55] And it is just as easy to interpret Debussy's setting of three of its poems between 1896 and 1898, in an interrelated triptych of *Chansons de Bilitis* (Songs of Bilitis), as his own small contribution to the erotic-exotic fascination Louÿs shared with countless contemporary artists.

Again, however, in the face of all interpretations of this triptych as an expression of the 'deep-seated sensualism . . . which stamped Debussy as a hedonist and sybarite' it is important to keep in mind the refined nature of his readerly talents.[56] Indeed, the allegorical accomplishment of the *Prélude à l'après-midi d'un faune* offers a useful point of reference in the attempt to understand this strangely diffident remark to Louÿs:

> Can you tell me what my three little 'musics' would add to a pure and simple hearing of your text? Nothing at all, my friend, I would even say that they would clumsily disperse the emotion of the hearers. What point is there, really, in fitting the voice of Bilitis here into major, there into minor, when she already has the most persuasive voice in the world? –You will say, 'Why have you made the music?' That, old chum, is another question . . . It is for other settings.[57]

This gnomic hint at a difference between songs written for direct emotional expression and those for 'other settings' offers an invitation to read through the 'pure and simple' prose of the *Chansons* to see if the 'most persuasive voice' of Bilitis, like that of Mallarmé's faun, bears subtler implications beneath its sensuous surface.

Having selected, to begin his triptych, two adjacent poems (nos. 30 and 31) from the first section of Louÿs's book, Debussy jumped, for his ending, to the last poem of the same section. The three chosen texts present a clear narrative progression. In the first, 'La flûte de Pan' (Pan's flute), a childlike Bilitis tells of her lessons in playing the pan pipes while seated on the lap of an unnamed male –

an activity whose sexual subtext is clear from her closing admission: 'My mother will never believe that I have stayed so long searching for my lost belt.' The second, 'La Chevelure' (The Hair), expresses a darker, more mature phase of sexual intimacy in a more roundabout fashion: Bilitis reports a dream 'he' told her, of becoming so entwined in her hair as they embraced that it seemed to be his; he became her; and she entered into him like his own dream. Her response to this 'tender' report – she lowers her eyes 'with a shudder' – is exquisitely ambiguous. 'Le tombeau des naïades' (The tomb of the naïads), finally, answers steamy oneiric passion with wintry scenes of loss and disillusionment. Bilitis, tracking satyrs through snowy forests, is told by an unnamed 'him' that the satyrs and nymphs have all perished from an extremely cold winter. In a final gesture, he breaks the ice of a spring 'where naïads used to laugh', and gazes through a shard at the pale sky.

Though deserving of Gide's 'Parnassian' epithet both for its antique imagery and its deceptively clear language, this prose poetry is not without its points of suggestive mystery. But while Debussy's settings abound in inspired responses to such details, the broader significance of the *Chansons* only emerges by considering the triptych as a continuous form – like the 'entire forest' of the faun poem – whose implicit narrative and diurnal progression (from evening to night to the 'day after') goes hand in hand with a deployment of musical materials just as studied as that in the *Prélude*. The kinship between the song triptych and the tone poem, with its famous opening flute solo, is signalled from the start: the first song begins with a sweeping, improvisatory arabesque, like a sweep of pan pipes across the lips, on one of the scales known as 'modes' Debussy and many contemporaries imported into modern music from more ancient practice. Then, as the voice flexibly declaims the first simple phrases, the piano accompaniment settles into euphonious oscillations between pure major triads (the fundamental building blocks of traditional harmony). When Bilitis's later reference to frogs singing at dusk receives a blatantly literal musical representation, we can recognize one more aspect of the song's deliberately 'naïve' musical stance (in the sense of Schiller's famous essay 'On Naïve and Sentimental Poetry'), which matches Bilitis's innocence with a prelapsarian euphony and representational simplicity.[58]

A delicately dissonant, sinuously coiling piano introduction darkens the tone for the second song. As 'she' reports 'his' dream over obsessively rocking accompaniments, Debussy's harmony relinquishes naïve triads and becomes clotted with dissonance. Leaving prelapsarian modes behind as well, voice and piano now interweave during the rise to passionate climax on one of Debussy's signature 'modern' scales.[59] A second, near-hysterical surge delivers at its peak one of those esoteric references to Wagner's *Tristan und Isolde,* before a final fade brings the piece to a close on a halting, dazed recollection of the opening. Finally, in the last song Debussy ratchets up the harmonic intensity one more step. Saturating his numbly plodding accompaniment with an even harsher dissonance he stretches yet further beyond 'La Chevelure' into the 'most advanced musical chemistry' (to borrow his own words on *La Saulaie*).[60] This third song ends on a dissonance whose resolution would be the home key of the first song – thus supporting the hint, within the triptych's linear narrative, of an eternally recurring diurnal 'cycle'.

Such an overview risks leaving the impression that Debussy merely made the most obvious choices: innocence received a naïve setting; dark passion a steamier one; wintry disillusionment the harshest of all. But we must not forget that he carved this little cycle out of Louÿs's disparate *Chansons,* thus raising into relief a triptych of texts that facilitated a three-stage musing, from the perspective of the 'sentimental' modern composer (to borrow again from Schiller), on ideals of musical expression. 'La flûte de Pan' embodies the antique-exotic ideal Debussy endorsed, at one point, when he claimed in the words of 'Monsieur Croche' to love 'those few notes from the flute of an Egyptian shepherd, [who] interacts with the landscape and hears harmonies unknown to our treatises'.[61] The text of 'La Chevelure,' by contrast, offered a compelling forum to activate those seductive powers he had celebrated in Wagner's *Tristan*: the music that 'embraces you like a caress' and makes you 'feel the same emotions as Tristan'.[62] (This association is sealed by the wrenchingly powerful nod to *Tristan* at the climactic words 'you entered into me like my dream'.) The more rebarbative setting of the third text – with its final image of a futile search, in frozen traces, for lost mythic ideals – can thus be taken as a markedly pessimistic answer to the central question for all ambitious avant-garde composers of Debussy's generation: What now, after the loss, alike, of antique-exotic idylls and Wagnerian dreams?

Debussy was to frame this question most succinctly a few years later when, in a note written for the *Opéra-Comique* entitled 'Why I wrote *Pelléas*', he suggested that Wagner 'had placed the full stop to the music of his times much in the way that Victor Hugo embraced all previous poetry. It was thus necessary to figure out how to be *after Wagner* [*après Wagner*] and not *after the manner of Wagner* [*d'après Wagner*].'[63] The *Chansons de Bilitis* triptych, far more than a straightforward translation of the exotic wet dreams of Debussy's friend Louÿs, stands alongside the Mallarmé *Prélude* as one of his most sophisticated enactments, through musical reading, of the question later encapsulated in that distinction between '*après*' and '*d'après*' Wagner. His distillation from the faun poem of a 'general rhythm' susceptible to projection through orchestral sound found its match, in this triptych, in his selection from Louÿs's book of three texts that could best allow him to rephrase that question through the 'persuasive voice' of Bilitis.

Signs of an Era's End

Debussy was to return twice more to that same voice: first, to write flute and harp accompaniments for a dramatic recitation of twelve more Bilitis poems in 1901; much later, to adapt some of those accompaniments in the 1914 set of *Six épigraphes antiques* for two pianos. Even though the 1898 triptych remains one of his greatest contributions to the song genre, this still seems a paltry handful of works to result from the countless exchanges with his friend about collaborative projects. But as one projected production of *Pelléas* after another foundered during these years, Louÿs was not the only aspiring collaborator to experience such frustration. The incidental music one of the original singers of *La Damoiselle élue* requested from Debussy in May 1896 to accompany a restaging of a play by Verlaine, for example, was not completed in time; nor was that sought by the caricaturist Jean-Louis Forain for a pantomime written by his wife. Meanwhile, numerous discussions with René Peter and Régine Dansaert for theatrical collaborations with Debussy also led nowhere.[64]

Such potential collaborators would likely have found little consolation in the fact that Debussy was making just as little headway with his independent projects. Having performed in the piano quartet by the recently deceased young Belgian composer Guillaume Lekeu at the Société nationale in January 1897, he vaguely proposed to the committee to write a new quartet and an oboe quintet.[65] No trace remains of either. More significant progress was made on the *Nuits Blanches*, a successor set to the *Proses lyriques* of songs on his own texts. But the fact that he made no effort to publicize either the five new poems or the two completed songs (unearthed in 1991) might suggest a recognition that the moment for such Symbolist posturing was passing.[66] Perhaps for a similar reason, Debussy abandoned an attempt to orchestrate the *Proses lyriques*, writing in March 1898 to Pierre de Bréville that 'I have changed my mind, and it now seems to me utterly useless to augment [these songs] with such an orchestral fracas.'[67]

The one work that Debussy did manage to complete for the Société during these years was just such an orchestral 'augmentation', of someone else's music. In February 1897, Gustave Doret conducted a programme that included two of Erik Satie's solo piano *Gymnopédies* in an orchestral arrangement by Debussy. Clearly undertaken primarily to publicize the music of his eccentric friend, this slight entry in Debussy's orchestral catalogue represented another foray into *faux*-antiquarian evocation. The hypnotic melodic and harmonic simplicity of Satie's bafflingly effective little pieces, which take their title from the ritual games of ancient Greek athletes, secured them a lasting place in the repertoire. In the long view, they anticipate the 'blank', timeless and objective vision of Classical antiquity that would, in such later works as the 1917 cantata *Socrate*, eventually win Satie belated pre-eminence as the figurehead for a post-Debussyan musical modernism. But while Debussy's orchestration might be said to infuse this marmoreal antiquarian vision with a more soft-edged 'naïveté' (as in 'La flûte de Pan'), we have no way of knowing how Satie evaluated the transformation, for we only retain letters between these two composers starting from much later, in 1903.[68]

If the span between the orchestration of the *Gymnopédies* and these letters testifies to the continuity from one century to the next of this one ill-documented friendship, the last years of the *fin de siècle* were also marked by the deaths of several key figures in Debussy's early development. His reaction to Verlaine's death in January 1896 went unrecorded, although it has been suggested that he joined the various Symbolist writers who gathered at the Batignolles cemetery in January 1897 for a mass in the poet's honour.[69] We know that he was present at another, strangely sepulchral Symbolist celebration the following month. After attending the banquet held for Mallarmé on the publication of his collected critical writings, Debussy commented witheringly to Louÿs about the 'rivalries, jealousies and petty exclusions' he encountered there, and confessed that 'I was prodigiously bored. M. seemed to share my opinion, and delivered, in a melancholy voice like Punchinello, a coldly constricted little speech.'[70] The sense of a literary era approaching its end was to be cruelly intensified a year and half later when Debussy learned of Mallarmé's sudden death. Writing to the poet's widow in September 1898, he expressed his 'real and intense sorrow' about 'the loss that Art in all its manifestations has just suffered'.[71]

Public marks of epochal change and rare compositional accomplishments aside, the growing list of abandoned or postponed projects delivered Debussy, by early 1898, to a nadir in his private hopes. Having expressed frustration in a letter to Hartmann of 31 December 1897 about 'a year in which I accomplished almost nothing that I wished', he then sank, by March, into an even more 'passionate' sadness that left him weeping (he confessed to Louÿs) as if 'this simple act, shared by all humanity, is the sole thing that remains to me within such anguish'. A month later, reaching the lowest point, he admitted: 'I hardly know where I am going, if it is not toward suicide, stupid ending for something that possibly merited better.'[72] Louÿs, who acknowledged once holding similar ideas himself, nonetheless responded with salutary bluntness:

> You, my friend, you do not have the shadow of an excuse for having such nightmares; because YOU ARE A GREAT MAN – do you know what that means? . . . Whatever troubles you are facing, this thought must dominate. You must continue your work and make it known, two things from which you have excused yourself and which should be everything for you. It is not by giving music lessons that you will secure your living, it is by doing everything possible to make sure *Pelléas* is performed.[73]

It is unclear how Debussy received this imperious grant of the same greatness Louÿs had previously assigned to Wagner. But soon enough he was to make crucial progress towards the performance of *Pelléas* that would prove a turning point in his career.

In late May 1898, Hartmann brought the new director of the Opéra-comique, Albert Carré, to Debussy's apartment to hear him play through *Pelléas et Mélisande*. The agreement then secured was the first concrete step towards the production of the opera under Carré's direction in 1902. But before the final practicalities could fall into place and the last revisions begin, Debussy had one more major composition – the most hard-won product of this crucial decade – to complete.

A More Grandiose Orchestral Allegory

Because of the long delay between the first 'completion' of *Pelléas* in 1895 and its 1902 premiere a historical account of Debussy's music through these years becomes somewhat tangled. If the *Chansons de Bilitis* effectively stand, compositionally speaking, one further step 'after Wagner' than the opera itself, yet another was taken in a much more grandiose project whose protracted creation, from 1897 through 1899, caused Debussy, he complained to Hartmann, 'more difficulty than the five acts of *Pelléas*'.[74] This project, which had its roots in the 'Nocturnes for principal violin and orchestra' proposed in 1894 to Ysaÿe (and abandoned due to his lukewarm response) eventually found public performance, in part in December 1900 and as a whole in November 1901, as the *Trois Nocturnes* for orchestra.

The three *Nocturnes*, which project the orchestral imagination of the *Prélude à l'après-midi d'un faune* through the triptych form of the *Chansons de Bilitis*, pose a greater interpretive challenge than either of these immediate precursors. Only one of the three – the last, *Sirènes* (Sirens), based on an episode in *The Odyssey* – can be securely tied to a poetic inspiration. The other two, *Nuages* (Clouds) and *Fêtes* (Festivals), bear titles vague enough to support the shallow imagistic associations that have largely forestalled consideration of the poetic implications of the whole. Indeed the learned critic Jean Marnold, who largely devoted his review of the 1901 premiere to tracing cyclic thematic cross-currents, launched a lasting tradition of formalist accounts when he dismissed as irrelevant to the work's permanent 'essence' both any hint of an extra-musical programme and whatever 'troubling emotion' it might seem to express.[75]

A first step towards a rehearing of this triptych in light of Debussy's allegorical and affective acuity would be to recognize the portentous weight of its one explicitly literary gesture. Given the cyclic unity Marnold outlined, the decision to close by evoking the famous 'sirens' episode in Homer's archetypical poem of wandering exile invites a search for related poetic resonances in the two previous nocturnes. In the case of *Nuages*, Debussy's first American biographer Oscar Thompson offered a suggestive hint when noting the importance of cloud imagery in the allegorical vocabulary of Baudelaire.[76] For example, in the famous first poem of the *Petits Poèmes en Prose*, 'L'Étranger', the eponymous stranger is asked what he loves: family; friends; homeland; gold. His negative responses inspire a final query:

> Then, what do you love, extraordinary stranger?
> I love the clouds . . . the clouds that pass . . . up there . . .
> up there . . . the wonderful clouds!

With this image in mind, we might well rehear the repeated cor anglais arabesque that drifts against dusky chord clouds in the first section of *Nuages* – a melancholy relative of the flute arabesque that marked the faun's ambivalence in his pastoral world – as a perfect melodic cipher of Baudelairean *anomie*.

At the heart of *Nuages*, the clouds part to reveal a contrasting musical vision featuring a stately melody for flute and harp using what was then called 'the Chinese scale'. Here again, it is easy to think of poetic precedents in the fine-brushed exotic idylls Baudelaire and Mallarmé often posed against the disillusionments of modern urban experience.[77] In this light, when the initial arabesque returns like the interruption of a dream before the piece's final 'grey agony' (to borrow from the original programme note), it is possible to glimpse poetic affinities between the questions raised by the first nocturne – a poignant musing on the promises of exotic fantasy, say – and the more explicit invocation of mythic exile in the third.[78]

Such a sense of unifying subtexts is strengthened by the more blatant musical symbolism of *Fêtes*. An initial rambunctious chain of 'tarantella' and 'saltarello' episodes vividly recalls the 'Italian carnival' trope previously featured in Mendelssohn's 'Italian' Symphony and Berlioz's 'Roman Carnival' overture. The whirling dances abruptly halt for a contrasting section whose play with perspective renders it one of Debussy's most blatantly programmatic episodes. A hushed march rhythm in strings and harp prepares the entry of the distant, muted trumpets of a military fanfare. Repeated louder and louder with larger and larger forces, the fanfare rises to overwhelming proximity just as the main tarantella theme returns – as if the military band has passed right through the festive dancing. At this pivotal crux of the triptych, the listener is thrust into the midst of a violent confrontation between militaristic fervour and carnivalesque frenzy. After a last blare of brass the whole fracas is cut short, leaving the fleet-footed dance rhythms to return – now pervasively tainted by echoes of trumpets and drums, all fading away into quizzical memories.

Sirènes, returning to the harmonic realm of *Nuages*, rounds off the triptych and offers a fraught summation. At the heart of the piece, after a long, becalmed passage of exquisitely delicate orchestration accompanying the wordless female choir that stands in for the deadly sirens, the mythical voices suddenly give way to impassioned strings for the triptych's only span of full-blooded Wagnerian lyricism. No sooner does this new 'voice' reach its peak than it, too, is cut off, leaving a plangent solo trumpet – a sound native to *Fêtes* – to state an arc of melody reminiscent of the cor anglais arabesque in *Nuages*. When the piece drifts to its close through a dim memory of the central, 'exotic' theme of *Nuages*, we are left with the sense of a subtly tangled concatenation of poetic and affective experiences.

To hear the final nocturne as a summation is not to say that it offers any clear answer to the preceding evocations. But the trumpet call seems an urgent invitation to reflect on the affective implications of the whole. Note, for a start, that the climactic march this single brass instrument summons in memory offers yet another ironic redeployment of *Tristan*-esqe harmonies – indeed an even more blatant and extensive reference to Wagner's chords than the knowing winks in the *Prélude* or the convulsive climax of 'La Chevelure'. Recalling the use of the same harmony to set Louÿs's words 'you entered into me like my own dream', the whole triptych can be said to pivot on a nod to *Tristan* whose scoring brings to mind Baudelaire's famous image of 'military bands pouring heroism into the hearts of the citizens'.[79] Indeed a few months after the 1901 premiere of the *Nocturnes* Debussy would invoke a similar image in his essay 'Music in the Open Air' when asking why 'military music' has gained a monopoly over 'squares and promenades', and suggesting in answer that such music totalizes a 'love of homeland [*la patrie*]' for everyone from a pastry chef to an 'old *monsieur* who thinks constantly of Alsace-Lorraine but never speaks of it'.[80]

While Debussy never explicitly identified a play with musical evocations of *la patrie* as a subtextual thread through the *Nocturnes*, this sense of a unifying undercurrent gives new resonance to the explicit clues he did offer, in a 1900 letter to Dukas, about one source of inspiration:

> I'll have you believe that the music of *Fêtes* was, as always, adapted from impressions already quite distant of a festival in the Bois de Boulogne; the 'chimerical procession' was, that day, made up of *cuirassiers* [horsemen in breastplate]![81]

Apparently, Debussy also told his lawyer friend Albert Poujaud that *Fêtes* was inspired by 'one of the first national festivals [*fêtes nationales*] given in Paris after the 70s'.[82] In Republican France, *fête nationale* means, precisely, the *quatorze juillet* (fourteenth of July) commemorations of the fall of the Bastille, first established in 1880 with a grand military assembly in the Bois de Boulogne.[83] Historians have noted an irresolvable tension in the attempts by early Republican leaders to impose such official 'national festivals' on a populace whose spontaneous 'popular' festivities were threateningly redolent of the revolutionary energies that had unseated various royal precursors.[84] A suggestive parallel emerges between, on the one hand, those press portrayals of *fin-de-siècle quatorze juillets* that juxtapose images of serried ranks in uniform with costumed dancers parodying authority, and on the other, the collision, in *Fêtes*, between an officious march music and a rambunctious offshoot of nineteenth-century 'carnivalesque' style.[85]

In short, it may be easy to decide with Marnold that the lasting value of the *Nocturnes* can be described in purely musical terms. But any attempt to understand the work as the product of the same sensibility behind the post-Wagnerian games in the *Prélude* and the *Chansons de Bilitis* brings to mind a swirl of hints to rehear it as an intricate chain of affective questions centring on the fantasies, aspirations and instabilities of early Republican nationhood. As a final twist, however, any rehearing of this work in these terms should also acknowledge that it was composed through the most intense years of the Dreyfus Affair – a national crisis that brought the Republican investment in *l'armée* as embodiment of *la nation* under severe strain. Precisely in the months that Debussy's torturous revisions were leading him to moan to Hartmann that 'the three *Nocturnes* are deeply affected by my life, and have been full of hope, then, full of despair and then full of emptiness!' the grossest poles of the Affair were being promulgated in pamphlets with such titles as '*La Nation et L'armée*' and '*L'Armée Contre la Nation*'.[86]

To see some significance in this coincidence of dates is not to identify the *Nocturnes* as a direct response to the Dreyfus trials. But a broader view might recognize how efficiently this work stands alongside the Affair in marking a pivotal point in the ideological evolution of a generation. For a writer like Debussy's exact contemporary Maurice Barrès, the fading embers of *fin-de-siècle* exoticism and *wagnérisme* would burn away in the furnace of Dreyfus-era debates, leaving behind a newly militant, proto-fascist version of nationalism. And while Debussy had been able in 1897 to sniff scornfully at the 'deplorable use of patriotism' in certain writings of Émile Zola and the composer Alfred Bruneau, the early years of the new century would see him tending more and more to

A poster commemorating the 1882 *fête nationale*, showing a typical *quatorze juillet* juxtaposition of military processions and carnivalesque entertainments.

a nationalist rhetoric that was ultimately to become just as chauvinistic as that of Barrès, if on a narrower musical terrain.[87]

Personal Changes

On a more mundane level, the same years saw equally convulsive developments in Debussy's domestic life. Some time in 1898 he had met an attractive young model, Lilly Texier, who initially sparked minimal interest. Subsequent meetings led rapidly to a new passion destined to displace Gaby Dupont from his life. A letter to Hartmann of January 1899 announcing Debussy's recent move to 58 rue Cardinet also reported that 'Mademoiselle Dupont, *my secretary*, has resigned her engagement.'[88] The reasons behind this dry conclusion of a seven-year relationship became clear a few months later in a sudden rush of letters to Lilly that could not contrast more starkly in tone. 'Claude is not yet cured of the bites from your dear little mouth!' exclaimed one of the first, in late April, before ending: 'impatient for your mouth, for your body, and for your love'.

When reading the correspondence of the next few months, it is startling to find just how far this reader of Baudelairean ironies and Mallarméan ideals could tumble into Romantic cliché:

> I cherish you right down to the habits that least please you about yourself: the One that one loves but once in life, the One who abolishes all the Past, the one who contains the desire to live within all that is most absolute, that is to say, the Happiness that is in the Beauty and the charm within everyday things.[89]

There may be some cause even at first reading to wonder just how long Debussy would remain satisfied with 'the charm within everyday things'. A more general question emerges about the near absence from these letters of any expression of shared aesthetic concern. A faint suspicion about Debussy's true compatibility with this latest paramour deepens in the face of one flippant note to Godet which both celebrates Lilly's 'fairy-tale prettiness' and notes her lack of interest in up-to-date musical developments.[90]

Such suspicion obviously derives from retrospective knowledge. At the time, Debussy was convinced enough to ask Lilly to marry him. Satie and Louÿs – who had recently married himself – were among the few witnesses present on 19 October 1899 at the civil ceremony, which was followed by a meal at the Taverne Pousset paid for in part by a piano lesson Debussy gave the same morning.[91] Here, finally, was the respectability he had once rashly sought with Thérèse Roger. Sadly, it came too late to mitigate his estrangement from Chausson, who had died in a bicycle accident only a few months before. But the liaison with Gaby ended civilly enough, for in the month of his marriage to Lilly Debussy gave her a copy of the manuscript of the *Prélude à l'après-midi d'un faune*, signed with the dedication 'To my dear and good little Gaby, the sure affection of her devoted Debussy'. Within months she too had moved on, ultimately to wed a wealthy South American banker.

A 1902 photograph of Debussy and his first wife Rosalie Texier, known as Lilly, whom he married in 1899.

A few months into married life, as the revisions to the *Nocturnes* and *Pelléas* continued, Debussy suffered the annoyance of another great success, with the opera *Louise*, by his *bête noire* Gustave Charpentier. Given its genre this popular triumph of a composer whose music he despised must have rankled even more than before. Interrupting his work, Debussy sent Hartmann another blast of invective about all 'realistic' (and 'nationalistic') posturing:

> He takes the 'Cries of Paris' which are rhythmically delicious and like a dirty Prix de Rome, he turns them into cantilenas at the moon and drags them into textbook harmonies! . . . Everything that is false and declamatory in the Aesthetic of 'beautiful roles' is contained in this work. Monsieur Mendès rediscovers Wagner in it, and Monsieur Bruneau discerns Zola. In sum: a truly French work. There has to be some mistake in the addition.[92]

In an almost identical missive to Louÿs Debussy further suggested that disillusionment with Parisian audiences was leading him to 'prefer it if *Pelléas* were played in Japan'.[93] But in truth, these same audiences were beginning, in these months, to grant Debussy a little more of the recognition he desired.

For one thing, the premiere of the *Chansons de Bilitis*, given in May 1900 by Debussy and Blanche Marot, received a laudatory review by one Gustave Bret, whose ears were fine enough to note that Debussy 'always leaves something implied, or half-expressed'.[94] Such refinement of response may still have been rare, but Debussy's place in Parisian musical life was nonetheless now prominent enough for his string quartet, *La Damoiselle élue*, and the *Chansons de Bilitis* to feature on the vast concert series of 'music from all over, of every kind' that rendered Paris a 'perpetual symphony' (as Dukas put it) during the International Exhibition of 1900.[95] All the same, he could only respond with bemusement at the cause of further delay in the public unveiling of his *Nocturnes*. Writing to Hartmann about the conductor's repeated decision to programme, instead, excerpts from Wagner's *Götterdämmerung* ('Twilight of the Gods') he quipped:

> As I see that Chevillard stubbornly persists in 'en-twilight-ing' his public, my poor *Nocturnes* are naturally left beneath the rubble, and I must remain broken-hearted, because I was much anticipating the joy that they would have given you. Oh well, everyone will have his turn . . . luck is essentially a portable thing.[96]

In one respect, this stoicism was to prove ill-founded. In a crueller irony than any temporary displacement of Debussy's latest music '*après* Wagner' by that of Wagner himself, his supporter Hartmann fell suddenly ill and was dead by the middle of May. If it is hard not to sense some selfishness in Debussy's response – 'I find the only editor capable of adapting himself to my delicious little soul', he wrote to Louÿs, 'and he has to go and die on me!!' – it is easy to sympathize with such a reaction to what must have seemed just one more of an endless stream of setbacks.[97]

In the end, while Hartmann was never to hear the *Nocturnes* the premieres of the first two in December 1900 and of the whole triptych about a year later garnered enough substantive critical recognition to stand as another pair of significant milestones in Debussy's career. In early 1901, furthermore, he gained a new public forum for the polemical battles he had previously fought only in private correspondence when he became music critic for *La Revue blanche*, a journal edited by the redoubtable art critic Félix Fénéon. All the while, Debussy's opera was inching its way towards the production that would secure him a measure of the fame that he would, in a last twist of irony, occasionally greet with just as much exasperation as the obscurity it was to replace.

3

The Art of a Curious Savage

Predictably enough, in the brief preamble that launched his first, short-lived stint as a music critic on 1 April 1901 Debussy disavowed any aspirations to conventional criticism. Claiming to offer only 'sincere impressions, honestly expressed', he dryly dismissed all highly technical appraisals:

> I will try to see, through musical works, the multiple movements that gave birth to them and all that they contain of the inner life; is that not more interesting than the game that consists of taking them apart like curious watches?[1]

Given his long-held distaste for textbooks and methods, such anti-analytical posturing is hardly surprising. But it also reflects a moment in which all musical study, particularly the technical aspect later institutionalized as 'Music Theory', was undergoing rapid professionalization. And when Debussy went on to disclaim any wish to comment on 'consecrated works' – which did not prevent him from writing about one of the most revered works of all, Beethoven's *Ninth Symphony* – it can be taken as a telling response to the consolidation, all around him, of the classical canon that was to become so central to twentieth-century musical culture.

Such broad cultural-historical hints aside, the pursuit of music's 'inner life' Debussy proceeded to offer both in his own voice and that of his alter ego 'Monsieur Croche' (a near-plagiaristic adaptation of

Paul Valéry's *fin-de-siècle* critical mouthpiece 'Monsieur Teste') arguably deserves the epithet 'Impressionistic' rather more than his compositions. Few opinions remain consistent from one acerbic offering to the next. Beyond vague proposals for a 'music of the open air' and a growing inclination to cultural nationalism – notably in polemical defences of the 'French' elegance of Jean-Phillippe Rameau – no systematic aesthetic emerges. Still, some entertainment value remains in the facility with anthropomorphic metaphor Debussy demonstrated, for example, when suggesting that in Massenet 'the harmonies resemble arms, the melodies necks; one leans over the brows of women in order to know, at all costs, what happens behind them'; or, elsewhere, that:

> The undeniable beauty of Liszt's oeuvre springs, I think, from the fact that he loved music to the exclusion of all other feeling. If, on occasion, he went so far as to address it familiarly and to place it squarely on his knees, that is no worse than the stuck-up manner of those who have the air of being presented to it for the first time.[2]

The cumulative effect of such imagery is a vivid, public version of the sardonic perspective on contemporary musical culture Debussy had long been expressing privately in his letters.

Occasionally he turned on more familiar bugbears. A celebration of Franck as one 'who serves music almost without demanding any glory', for example, provided a foil for one of many snarls at Wagner: 'when he borrows from life, he dominates it, puts his foot on top of it and forces it to cry the name of Wagner more loudly than the trumpets of fame.'[3] The persistence of such jabs demonstrates the degree to which Debussy's relations with this particular precursor remained unresolved even after the production of *Pelléas et Mélisande* had secured him significant fame on Wagner's own ground. But while the agonistic layers of post-*wagnériste* response seem an unavoidable subtext to all discussions of *Pelléas*, it could be that the opera is best approached, in the first place, through the prism of Debussy's words on one of the few composers who appears in letters and criticism alike in a uniformly positive light.

On 15 April 1901 Debussy gave the readers of *La Revue Blanche* his warmest praise of a favourite Russian alternative to faded *wagnériste* passions. In an effusive review he celebrated Mussorgsky's little cycle of songs on poems from a child's perspective, *The Nursery*, in terms that could not be more illuminating of his own ideals as he nursed his opera towards completion:

> Never has a more refined sensibility been translated by such simple means; it resembles the art of a curious savage who would reveal the music within each step traced by his emotion; nor is it ever a question of some form or other, or at least this form is so multifarious that it is impossible to relate it to established – we might say administrative – forms; it is composed by small successive touches, connected by a mysterious thread and by a gift of luminous clairvoyance.[4]

Here, in short, is a paean to the simplicity Debussy would repeatedly affirm as his artistic ideal in the face of disgruntlement about his Byzantine intricacies. Here too is a perfect image for his vision of a dramatic music that, rather than indulging in tired conventions of expansive lyricism – in which the gap between dramatic and musical emotions, he suggested, makes characters 'sit on a note to allow the music to catch up' – instead tracks the fluctuations of 'inner life' step by step like a 'curious savage'. And here, finally, is the perfect description of the operatic style that emerged from his rejection not only of conventional forms, but also traditional phrasing: a music of 'small, successive touches, connected by a mysterious thread'.

As it turned out not everyone who first experienced *Pelléas* some months later readily granted Debussy the same 'luminous clairvoyance' he attributed to Mussorgsky. But before tracing the last steps to the opera's 1902 production and sampling the critical reaction it is worth pausing to take particular note that this extravagant praise greeted a collection of songs that gives voice to the perspective of a child. Over the ensuing decade the theme of childhood, in implicit or explicit tension with elusive ideals of maturity, would rise to new prominence alongside Debussy's other preoccupations. Indeed, in considering the degree to which *Pelléas* not only fulfils his early ambitions to 'clothe the poetry, in order to convey the sense of something truly lived' but also approaches the more sophisticated literary responses of the *Prélude* and the Louÿs songs, attention to this particular theme can aid an attempt to thread the maze of Maeterlinck's symbolism and evaluate Debussy's grandest single act of compositional reading.

Last Steps to the Stage

Throughout the year 1901, as Debussy saw his first articles into print and, later, absorbed reactions to the first complete performance of all three *Nocturnes* (received as a triumph by Dukas, the triptych occasioned one of many cautions against seductive Debussyan 'sorcery' from the influential critic Paul Lalo), his compositional activity remained relatively sparse. One minor work, the musical accompaniment for flutes, harps and celesta he wrote for a recitation with danced *tableaux vivants* of twelve more poems from the book of *Chansons de Bilitis*, offered a far less refractory engagement with the antique exoticism of Louÿs's poetry than the earlier song triptych. A couple of months later, Debussy made sure Louÿs was one of the first to receive the latest news from the director of the Opéra-Comique: 'Because you are, in spite of everything . . . my old friend Pierre! I do not want you to learn from someone else that: *I have the written promise from M. Alfred Carré that he will stage Pelléas et Mélisande next season.*'[5]

Whatever it may have owed to their latest Bilitis collaboration, this warm reaffirmation of friendship probably also reflects some sense of Louÿs's proprietary interest in the opera given his key role as mediator with Maeterlinck almost ten years before. On that terrain, however, one last setback was still to unfold. During the few months that remained before the premiere the playwright, once graciously accommodating to Debussy's plans, turned violently against the opera.

The main point of contention concerned Maeterlinck's presumption that the role of Mélisande should be created by his mistress Georgette Leblanc. As evidenced by the legal documents drafted at the hearing that adjudicated Maeterlinck's attempt to reclaim his play, Debussy did not reject this idea outright but ceded the final decision to Carré. The director later recalled that he had been in no doubt of Leblanc's talents – indeed he would cast her in Dukas's 1907 Maeterlinck opera *Ariane et Barbe-Bleue* – but felt he had previously erred in giving her the lead in Bizet's *Carmen* and wished to avoid a similar mistake with *Pélléas*. Beautiful as Leblanc may have been, he elaborated diplomatically, she 'did not possess the physical qualities of the woman-child character that was Mélisande'. These, as it happened, were qualities he had already found miraculously conjoined in the Scottish soprano Mary Garden, just then enjoying considerable success in Charpentier's *Louise*.[6]

Carré's reference to Mélisande's 'woman-child character' opens a window on this opera's lasting challenges to singers and critics alike. By contrast, the terms with which Maeterlinck excoriated the work once his claim had been dismissed and rehearsals proceeded seem bizarrely out of line with later assessments. Soon after attending an open rehearsal on 19 March 1902 he sent a scathing open letter to the weekly journal *Le Figaro*:

> They succeeded in excluding me from my own work, and since then it has been treated as a conquered territory. They have

> undertaken arbitrary and absurd cuts which render it incomprehensible; they have retained all that I intended to suppress or improve . . . In a word, the *Pelléas* in question has become a piece that is strange to me, almost an enemy; and stripped of all control over my work, I am reduced to wishing that it suffers prompt and resounding failure.[7]

Whether or not we accept the explanation Maeterlinck's friend Octave Mirbeau offered Carré – the playwright, he suggested, was suffering a madness inspired by 'the evil genius of a woman' – it remains striking just how radically this complaint departs from the general view of *Pelléas* as an opera exceptionally (even excessively) faithful to the original play.[8] Long before any critical tradition developed, the composer Richard Strauss put this point most archly when he grumbled on hearing the opera for the first time in 1907: 'there is not enough music for me, here. These are very fine harmonies, very good orchestral effects; but this is nothing, nothing at all. I find that it is nothing more than Maeterlinck's play, all alone, without music.'[9]

The gulf between the two responses reflects fundamentally different priorities. Woman-crazed or not, Maeterlinck reacted with an author's understandable preciosity when discovering that one of his works had been subject to extensive cuts. On the other hand Strauss, Wagner's leading heir on the grounds of lushly orchestrated, mythopoetically grandiose opera, could hardly have found much to admire in this work's determined avoidance of all he thought essential to 'musical phrases' and 'development'.[10] Somewhere between the two responses can be found a judicious appraisal of the opera: a product both of a literary sensibility that, while scrupulously faithful to Maeterlinck's prose rhythms, saw the need for numerous surgical excisions to tighten his dramatic form; and a musical aesthetic that, in service of a stringent ideal of 'natural' declamation, brought to the stage the new understanding of the musical phrase Debussy had long been honing in his songs.

A Play and an Opera

In the same little book in which he recorded those 1889 conversations with Guiraud, Debussy's erstwhile Conservatoire colleague Maurice Emmanuel briefly summarized *Pelléas et Mélisande*:

> An old king, Arkël, in a legendary time and country; his son, ill, hidden in some corner of the palace; his two grandsons, Golaud, the elder, and Pelléas; their mother, Genevieve; an unknown woman, who will marry Golaud and love Pelléas . . . The plot is one of the simplest of all: an old husband, 'because it is the custom' kills the lover of his young wife. She also dies, and forgives him. But . . . 'what is there to forgive?' The murderer will never really know whether or not his vengeance was justly taken.[11]

This sketchy précis efficiently captures a central duality of the work. In outline, this 'simplest plot' – a love triangle – may indeed seem (as musicologist Joseph Kerman later noted) 'oddly conventional'.[12] But rather less so is the bafflement that accumulates through the elliptical exchanges between characters. Ultimately, in spite of the 'old husband' Golaud's desperate search for truth both he and the audience are left in doubt about the most basic question of all, concerning the precise kind of love his wife Mélisande and his young brother Pelléas actually shared.

Of the many excisions that brought the play even closer to Debussy's ideal libretto, several reinforced the theme of a vain search for truth. By removing the first scene of servants washing the castle steps, for example, he effectively plunged his audience directly from the antique-flavoured orchestral prelude into the murky forest of Allemonde with Golaud. The opera's first utterance – having lost his way while hunting, Golaud sighs 'I will never be able to get out of this forest' – thus gains relief as a motto for the whole experience about to unfold. At the same time, the excision of this and three other full scenes recast Maeterlinck's overall dramatic shape into new formal symmetries – for example, between the three-scene Acts I and II.

This broadest reshaping may seem enough cause for the playwright's fury. But Debussy also pruned just about every scene he retained. While dispensing with excessive exposition and repetition, his scalpel may also have been guided by a reaction against what one critic had termed a 'pointless abundance of symbols, at times too simplistic, and at times too blatant'.[13] Countless references to light and dark and blind or unreliable eyes recur in blatant association with the theme of truth-seeking. Almost as pervasive is the water imagery: the first meeting of Pelléas and Mélisande occurs overlooking the sea; later they meet twice at a well, once leading to the loss of her wedding ring, the other culminating in their one brief love scene. Such instances might seem all too easy to read from a post-Freudian perspective. But at times, the symbolic cross-currents combine with more multivalent richness – as when two central scenes juxtapose the 'water of death' in the castle vaults against the life-giving water Pelléas sees on emerging into breezy brilliance, sprinkling over gardens to the sound of 'children running down to the beach to bathe'.

Even after Debussy's surgery such symbolic interplay renders any pursuit of interpretive solidity like an attempt 'to carry water in a muslin bag' (to borrow an image from the opera). Still, some consensus has emerged that the opera's central 'lesson' can be taken to be, in the words of one early critic, that 'fate governs the world, that events drive us forward and that all resistance is vain, on our part, against the secret laws of destiny'.[14] When distilled down to such flaccid generality it is easy to understand why some have complained of dramatic weakness. But while the emphasis on fate may be easy to justify with reference to the gloomy pronouncements of the old king Arkël, as a general proposition it

Scottish soprano Mary Garden photographed in the role of Mélisande, *c.* 1902, showing a hint of the 'woman-child character' noted by director Albert Carré.

tends to foreclose inquiry into the ways the play might enfold more precise significance.

It helps to recall the seemingly trivial fact that Emmanuel's summary begins by demarcating chain of generations: 'an old king . . . his son . . . his grandsons . . . their mother'. As stated, the chain is incomplete, for Golaud already has a son, Yniold, by a previous marriage; his new wife will bear a daughter before her death. Maeterlinck does not demarcate every link in the chain clearly.[15] But he continually positions his characters against an ever-present lattice of stages of the life cycle. Fatefully ineluctable as the progression through this cycle may seem, it is the dramas of identity posed at its discrete stages that provide a humane core of empathy to which Debussy's music proved a particularly telling supplement.

The extremes are most clearly defined. Arkël attributes his fatalistic wisdom to his proximity to death; Debussy wrote of his struggle to infuse one scene with 'the compassion of a child to whom a sheep gives at first the idea of a toy that he cannot touch, and also a pity that people concerned with their comfort no longer possess'.[16] In between these poles lies the shifting terrain occupied by 'people concerned with their comfort' – that is, the realm of maturity so precariously upheld by Golaud. And the catalyst that pushes precariousness over the edge of tragic failure is the 'unknown woman', Mélisande, who will not sit still on the ladder of maturity. The phenomenon recalls a comment in Maeterlinck's mystical essay 'On Women':

> [Women] are truly the veiled sisters of all the great things we cannot see. They are truly the close relatives of the infinite that surrounds us and they, alone, know how to smile at it with the familiar grace of the child who does not fear its father.[17]

The image of 'the child who does not fear its father' is literally relevant to one scene in which Golaud uses Yniold as an informant about the relationship between Pelléas and Mélisande. But it also captures Golaud's inability, in spite of ongoing attempts – 'you are no longer a child'; 'you are no longer at the age to cry over such things' – to claim Mélisande for his 'mature' stage of the life cycle. At the same time, his contradictory tendency to dismiss her dalliances with Pelléas as 'childish games' seems particularly obtuse when, for example, he finds her leaning from a window with Pelléas ecstatically tangled in her hair. The same incomprehension recurs in the final scene: having slain Pelléas, Golaud blames himself at Mélisande's deathbed for 'killing without reason' since 'they had embraced like little children . . . they were brother and sister'.

Debussy's setting of all these scenes deepens the sense of an unbridgeable gulf between 'mature' and 'child-like' perspectives.

At the beginning of Act III scene iv, Golaud, placing Yniold on his knees, interrogates him about his time in the company of his new 'mummy' and uncle Pelléas. His fury at the child's blandly literal replies drives him to a violent gesture. When he attempts to assuage the boy's hurt with a bribe the music, which has been closely tracking the darkly perverse undertones, pinpoints the gulf between father and child: a tiny window of naïve, light-fingered simplicity marks the degree to which Yniold, captivated by the promised bow and arrow, remains impervious to his father's obsession. This is but a foretaste of the much lengthier musical deflection when Golaud forces the interrogation to its climax: 'Do they sometimes kiss?' 'No' answers the boy – but then corrects himself: 'yes, once, when it was raining.' Sensing truth at his fingertips, Golaud asks *how* they kiss, only to receive a playful kiss himself – 'Like this, daddy, like this' – and a blithe bit of chatter, over whimsically cheerful music, about his prickly beard and grey hair. Although Golaud will try again to pin down the truth, the stark juxtaposition of musical worlds marks his search as futile even before a last crescendo of aggression brings the scene to its close.

Trivial as it might seem, Yniold's reference to Golaud's hair and beard echoes Mélisande's equally naïve reaction to Golaud's age during the very first dialogue of the opera. The most telling outgrowth of this parallel in childish perspectives occurs in the final scene. Golaud, left alone with his dying wife, makes one last reach for the truth. When the initial, affirmative answer to his plea for forgiveness disconcertingly becomes a question set to angelically sweet accompaniment – 'what is there to forgive?' – it is clear that their interaction is to unfold between incommensurate worlds of understanding. As in the scene between father and child, where the verb *embrasser* (to kiss) could mean either romantic or familial embrace, the dialogue comes to pivot on the ambiguity of a single word, *aimer*, to love. When Golaud finally blurts the question 'Did you love Pelléas?' she blithely answers 'yes' over a moment's silence in the orchestra – only for a coolly ethereal harp and horn to usher in the gentle flute tones that colour her next words: 'I loved him. Where is he?'

Realizing that she has not grasped his meaning, Golaud again lurches onto crudely literal terrain: 'I am asking you whether you loved with a forbidden love. Were you guilty? Tell me, tell me, yes, yes.' Accompanied by a delicate flute halo and a heavenly high violin, her response – 'no, we were not guilty, why do you ask that?' – exposes yet another maddening misunderstanding. For Golaud, guilt is a state of being that results logically from 'forbidden' acts; for Mélisande, it is an emotion one may or may not have felt.

Some have heard such responses as the manipulative deceptions of a mature 'woman character'. But in view of Mélisande's resistance to clear definition it is better to let this culminating ambiguity about love inform retrospective reflection about the 'love scene' that precipitated Golaud's fatal intervention. In the last scene of Act IV, as Pelléas and Mélisande meet at the well on the night before his departure from Allemonde, he finally blurts his confession: 'I love you.' The extreme restraint of her muted reply – 'I love you too', whispered on a single note over a breathless orchestral hush – has often been celebrated as the opera's most iconically anti-lyrical moment. But her faint declaration does, in fact, trigger an extravagantly lyrical outburst from Pelléas – the closest thing to a Massenet aria in the opera.

Perhaps this is the point at which Debussy's strictures about musical and dramatic emotion fell away in favour of a full, heart-on-sleeve concession to traditional melodic expectations. But the disappointment some have felt about the love scene is understandable in view of this naïve reaction to Mélisande's faint echo of a word (*aimer*) whose instability she is soon to expose. Recalling Debussy's self-conscious treatment of Romantic lyricism in his contemporaneous works, we might well ask whether there is

PELLÉAS ET
MÉLISANDE

CLAUDE DEBUSSY
MAURICE MAETERLINCK

Frontispiece of Maeterlinck's libretto for *Pelléas et Mélisande*, showing the moment of amorous abandon by the fountain and the spying Golaud.

something ironic, 'in quotes' – like the Bellini-esque bel canto at the heart of the *Prélude à l'après-midi d'un faune* – about the Romantic outpouring he gives to Pelléas at this most intimate moment of his opera.

Still, it would not do to resolve Mélisande's identity too clearly in the childish direction either. She finds her own version of Romantic passion when, in response to Pelléas's recognition that they have been locked out of the castle, she leaps into his arms with a cry: 'All the better!' It is crucial, in short, to recall that even with the meticulous rhythms and expressive inflections Debussy gave to Maeterlinck's 'woman-child character', there remains a great deal about her he could never pin down in a musical score. Perhaps he offered a sly clue to the challenge for all aspiring Mélisandes when in 1903, exceptionally for this phase of his career, he set a single poem, 'The Garden', by a minor poet, Paul Gravollet. It is hard to see what attracted him to this precious little text if it was not some hint of recognition in its description of 'a grown girl and yet childlike / Cunning only by instinct'. And if this song, with its references to hair and 'eyes shaded by long lashes' and 'frail and charming body', might be taken as a wry after-image of the 'woman-child character' in his opera, perhaps one clue to resolving the challenge Mélisande perpetually poses in her poise between naiveté and sexual allure is to be found in Gravollet's succinct formulation: 'voice of April, but gestures of May'.

A Production and its Aftermath

In terms of scale and public impact, *Pelléas et Mélisande* remains Debussy's single most significant act of compositional reading. But in any judicious view, Strauss's crotchety overstatement about 'Maeterlinck's play . . . without music' bears a hint of valid insight. Even with due regard for his editorial interventions, Debussy's broadly respectful treatment of the play renders *Pelléas* a more straightforward reading than the *Prélude à l'après-midi d'un faune*, whose orchestral translation of Mallarmé required several inspired imaginative leaps, or the *Chansons de Bilitis*, whose allegorical progression was a product of the composer's shaping intelligence. Maeterlinck's play, set in 'Allemonde' (a German-French hybrid implying 'all-the-world'), came with portentous allegorical ambitions in plain view. If Debussy's 'successive touches' of orchestral colour and delicate melodic 'cantilena' (as Emmanuel called it) amounted to a strikingly unfamiliar style of opera, he nonetheless did little to transform the play's 'lessons' – whether these hinge on a general idea of fate or on threatened ideals of maturity and truth in a time of social upheaval.[18]

It could even be argued that *Pelléas* does not present his most distinctive negotiation with 'music after Wagner'. To be sure, as Carolyn Abbate demonstrated long ago, while he took pains to erase some blatant echoes of *Tristan und Isolde* in the love scene he left the opera strewn with those more esoteric Wagnerian references familiar from his contemporary works.[19] But when suffused through Maeterlinck's symbolic web across over two hours of finely shaded orchestral tapestry, such harmonic winks seem less freighted than they do in the more formally compact Mallarmé *Prélude* and Louÿs songs – let alone the blazingly powerful march in *Fêtes*. Indeed, for Debussy's later partisan Boulez no less than his grouchy contemporary Strauss, any esoteric dialogue with *Tristan* proved less significant than the opera's audible debts to *Parsifal* – the Wagnerian music drama that remained a touchstone for Debussy's orchestral thinking to the end of his life.

Needless to say, the public that first heard the work in April and May 1902 were not concerned with such fine distinctions. The final steps to the stage had been far from smooth. Although the conductor André Messager quickly won over the cast, the problems encountered during the many orchestral rehearsals were so daunting that Debussy, as late as March 1902, announced to René Peter that he would withdraw the work.[20] The limited scenic resources of the Opéra-Comique, which made the numerous set changes impracticable, required a late, hasty expansion of several orchestral interludes. Even as he undertook these last revisions Debussy became embroiled in negotiations with the set painters that seemed like a battle towards imperfect understanding. Once all these dimensions had finally been shepherded to the open rehearsal on 28 April, he found that some ill-wisher had manoeuvred for Maeterlinck's desired failure by distributing a derisory pamphlet. Thus primed, many in the audience found ready excuse for mockery in Mélisande's pathetically prosaic complaint – 'I am not happy here' – at the end of Act II, and in Yniold's grating repetitions of 'Daddy' in the spying scene (which had exasperated Debussy himself).

As Messager recalled, the power of the fourth and fifth acts won over enough supporters to balance the protesters by the final curtain.[21] But the division of opinion carried over into the critical reception. On one hand, enough commentators echoed a complaint about 'lack of melody' that Debussy saw fit to insist in a tetchy 'response to the critics' that 'melody, if I may say so, is almost anti-lyrical. It is powerless to translate the mobility of souls and of life.'[22] On the other hand, Maeterlinck's pique could hardly have been assuaged by Dukas's ringing praise for:

> A music so naturally incorporated into the action, so naturally arising from the situation, from the decor and the language, a music so closely reunited with the music included in the words that, within the total impression produced by the sonorous transfusion, it becomes impossible to dissociate it from the text that it penetrates; to the extent that in the final analysis it might appear just as much the unconscious work of the poet as the poem is that of the musician.[23]

While it may have been easy to dismiss Dukas as a committed partisan, it would have been harder to undermine the praise of Pierre Lalo, a more ambivalent critic, who nonetheless took *Pelléas* as the decisive illustration of the degree to which 'all is poetry, just as all is music, in [Debussy's] oeuvre; and all his music is poetry'.[24]

Still, in spite of the enthusiasm of such influential commentators, any decisive evaluation of the opera's success can only be a historical simplification. The fact that Boulez could write in 1969 of the work's 'failure with audiences' reflects its entanglement in the questions about esotericism Debussy had been courting since the early 1890s – as Emmanuel noted when paraphrasing the question of another critic: 'Is this not a language a bit too distant and aristocratic, which risks remaining incomprehensible to the non-initiated?'[25] For aficionados of the 'beautiful singing' of operatic divas the answer can only be 'yes'. But for those composers (from Dukas to Bartók and Berg and beyond) who sought ways to sustain this pre-eminent genre of the nineteenth century into the twentieth, *Pelléas et Mélisande* was to prove an inexhaustible source of inspiration.

For Debussy the production proved both personally and professionally pivotal. Soon after accompanying Messager in London in July 1902, Debussy wrote to him affirming their new, profound friendship in terms that touch both the theme of childhood and the crucial ambiguity in the opera's final act:

> There are things about which I have never spoken except with you, which makes me find your friendship precious to such a point that I do not know how to say enough about it . . . Do not find this too childish a story because the sentiment about which I am speaking is perhaps more elevated than Love.[26]

The new friendship with Mary Garden, though less intense, was to leave an invaluable trace in the recordings of songs and excerpts

A suburban gathering around the time of the premiere of *Pelléas et Mélisande* in 1902. From left to right: the lawyer Paul Poujaud, Debussy, the critic Pierre Lalo (seated), Lilly Debussy and the composer Paul Dukas.

from *Pelléas* she made with Debussy in 1904 for the French record company *Le Gramophone*. But of all the new connections stimulated by the opera the most significant was to spring from a positive review published in *La Revue musicale* in November 1902. When he gratefully invited the review's author for a personal meeting Debussy inaugurated one of the most important relationships of his later years. Indeed, the friendship with the young musicologist Louis Laloy – which bore immediate fruit in the honour of 'Chevalier de la Légion d'Honneur' granted to him by the state in January 1903, in part due to Laloy's machinations – was to be one of the few, new or old, to survive the turbulence that soon engulfed his personal life.

Professionally speaking, in spite of Debussy's cynicism about the tendency to measure artistic success in box-office terms – 'to have made *Pelléas* is of mere anecdotal significance, but to make good receipts, that's the main thing!' – he seems to have seen his opera as the long-sought key to material prosperity, for he initially retained the publication rights himself.[27] Even as he plunged into laborious preparation of the proofs the eagerness with which he turned to fresh projects can be taken as evidence of a kind of creative release. The first substantial glimpse of a new literary preoccupation appeared in August 1902 in a letter to Messager announcing intensive work on Edgar Allan Poe's tale 'The Devil in the Belfry'. But while Debussy confessed apprehension about public reactions to this abandonment of 'the shadows of Mélisande for the ironic pirouette of the Devil', such fears were to prove ill-founded for the simple reason that neither this work nor the later project on Poe's 'The Fall of the House of Usher', which were to occupy him sporadically for the rest of his life, ever reached completion.

Ill-starred readings of Poe aside, the years 1903–4 were creatively significant both for the works Debussy saw into print and the much more extensive list of projects he contracted for future publication. Not all were entirely the products of his own personal inclinations. A letter to his wife of 31 May 1903 contains a first reference to the 'woman with the saxophone', Elisa Hall (president of the Orchestral Club of Boston), who was seeking new works for the instrument she had taken up at the age of forty-seven.[28] Although Debussy was to work on his saxophone *Rhapsody* off and on for several years, his failure to finish the orchestral version – ultimately completed posthumously by a colleague – undoubtedly had something to do with his unfamiliarity with the 'habits' of this particular 'reed animal'.[29] But this project also clearly paled in interest beside the more personal vision for a series of works under the collective title *Images*. Although some vagueness remained about musical forces (the pieces were to be for solo piano and 'two pianos or orchestra'), the fact that the poetic titles specified for nine out of twelve works in the initial contract of 8 July 1903 survived almost unchanged into the two sets of *Images* for piano (1905–8) and the *Images* for orchestra (1905–12) testifies to the clarity of Debussy's original vision. Just as clear in outline if not in detail, finally, was another vision for a grand orchestral triptych based on his 'countless memories' of the sea, first announced to Messager in September.[30] When completed in 1905, *La Mer* was to prove his grandest masterpiece after *Pelléas*.

By the end of 1903, in short, most of the works that would preoccupy Debussy over the next several years were either under way or clearly in view. The one significant new composition to appear in print, furthermore, can be seen as a crucial breakthrough in a musical medium so far oddly marginal to his compositional explorations. Back in 1901, the publication of the triptych *Pour le piano* had marked the appearance of the first of Debussy's works for his own instrument that retains a secure place in the virtuoso repertoire. But as his younger contemporary Maurice Ravel later respectfully observed, this showy, prosaically titled set offers little evidence of a distinctive Debussyan pianistic voice.[31] It was only after Ravel's *Jeux d'eau* appeared in 1902 that Debussy completed a triptych for solo piano, under the collective title *Estampes* ('prints'), whose progression through three evocative panels – *Pagodes, La Soirée dans Grenade, Jardins sous la pluie* – belatedly matched the sonorous poetry long apparent in his songs and orchestral works.

A 'Bad Outcome'?

While Debussy was destined to complete most of the projects envisioned in the years immediately after *Pelléas*, it would be misleading to see his aesthetic evolution through this time as simple or straightforward. As the musicologist Guido Gatti noted in 1920, 'the personality of Debussy is one of those which unfolded in concentric circles'.[32] A clear exemplification of this non-linear evolution can be seen in the two song triptychs he completed in 1904.

First of all, in the second of two song cycles on poems from Verlaine's collection *Fêtes galantes*, Debussy offered his last readings of a key early literary inspiration. This second, 1904 *Fêtes galantes* triptych ends by pointedly recalling a birdlike arabesque for piano that had long ago, in Debussy's 1891 triptych of the same name, been associated with the archetypical Romantic image of the nightingale. The valedictory weight of the recollection in 'Colloque Sentimentale' is clear from Verlaine's words about two aged 'spectres' who walk together in a frozen landscape evoking a shared Romantic past. The emotional gulf between the one who wishes to remember and the one who does not is captured in starkly contrasting language:

> - Do you remember our former ecstasy?
> - Why do you want me to remember it?
> - Does your heart still beat merely at my name?
> Do you still see my soul in your dreams? - No.
>
> - Ah! Those beautiful days of inexpressible happiness
> When we joined our lips together! - It is possible.
> - How blue was the sky, and how great our hope!
> - Hope has fled, vanquished, into the black sky.

Pacing the melodic declamation of this dialogue just as finely as he had the exchanges in Maeterlinck's play and colouring the exquisitely spare accompaniment with fleeting surges of radiant, post-Wagnerian harmony, Debussy's setting of this 'sentimental colloquy' bids a poignant farewell to Romantic lyricism.

Years later, he was to echo the same Romantic cliché when suggesting that 'it is not necessary to hear the song of the nightingale, that of the locomotive responds better to modern artistic preoccupations'.[33] But in truth, his negotiations with and against the Romantic heritage would never lead to significant flirtation with 'machine aesthetics'. In fact, during the first decade it is possible to discern a growing alienation from the radical experiments of the next generation. A visit to the 1908 *Salon d'Automne* – a forum for the most advanced painting – was to leave him complaining that 'these people, who I would like to believe lack spitefulness, are strenuously trying to disgust everyone including themselves (one must hope) with painting'.[34] Around the same time, a letter to the writer Georges Jean-Aubry provided an occasion to gripe about 'contemporary poets' who extract 'fraught lyricism from direly mediocre subject matter'.[35]

This sense of a gradual falling out of step with radical developments provides perspective on the fact that Debussy (unlike Ravel, for example, in the 1905 *Histoires naturelles* on texts by Jules Renard) did not turn to a contemporary poet to refresh his post-Romantic song-writing. Instead, he turned to a more distant past. The triptych *Trois Chansons de France*, also published in 1904, features settings of two *rondels* by the fifteenth-century nobleman Charles d'Orléans alongside a single setting of the seventeenth-century poet Tristan l'Hermite.[36] This reach back into the depths of French literary tradition can be seen as further symptom of the nationalism Debussy was exemplifying most clearly, in these years, in his critical polemics on behalf of Rameau.

The adoption of an 'antique' style of poetry affected the musical style of the songs. The deft treatments of the highly repetitive refrain structures of the d'Orléans *rondels* may distantly recall the similar imaginative play with musical recall in his much earlier settings of Baudelaire. But now, the games with textual and musical recall are projected through a studied pose of melodic and accompanimental simplicity. The only point at which some of the old, blood-rich Baudelairean languor re-emerges (for l'Hermite's poem about 'a dark grotto / where . . . The tide struggles against the pebbles, / And light against shadow') remains a paler, more stately version of the post-Wagnerian grandeur now lost to the past.

This 'archaeological' turn from the faded legacy of Symbolism to the depths of French literary history was to prove more than a momentary indulgence, for Debussy would choose similarly antiquated texts for most of his later songs. But if it is thus clear that the farewell to Romantic lyricism in *Fêtes galantes II* must be understood, aesthetically speaking, as a backward-looking turn, at the same time this triptych, when published, bore explicit hints of new developments in Debussy's personal life. On sending the proofs for the songs to the editor Durand in July 1904 he specified that the dedication was to read: 'In gratitude for the month of June 1904', followed by the letters 'A. l. p. M.' Admitting that this might seem 'a little mysterious,' he suggested that 'it is necessary to make some contribution to legend'.[37]

The 'legend' in question was to arise around one of the most convulsive dramas of Debussy's personal life. 'A. l. p. M.' stands for '*à la petite mienne*', meaning 'to my dear little one'. This was Debussy's affectionate nickname for Emma Bardac, the married mother of one of his students, with whom he had recently embarked on a passionate affair. Indeed, he sent the *Fêtes galantes* proofs from the Grand Hotel in Jersey, where he was secretly staying with Emma.[38] Their late-summer tryst in Jersey and Dieppe was the culmination of a connection that had been growing since, upon first meeting her in June 1903, he had dedicated a copy of the recently revised *Ariettes oubliées* to her with the words 'to Madame S. Bardac whose musical sympathy is precious to me – infinitely'. Clearly, in Emma – an accomplished singer for whom Gabriel Fauré had composed his song cycle *La Bonne Chanson*, and who had been performing Debussy's songs since the late 1890s – he had found a partner whose fine attunement to his own *métier* promised much broader sympathy than the physical passions that had once drawn him to Lilly.

Debussy at Pourville on the Normandy seaside in 1904, during the trip with Emma Bardac that preceded his divorce from Lilly.

A clear indication of this new level of connection can be seen in a postcard Debussy sent to Emma in June 1904 bearing no message beyond a hand-written citation of 'Le faune', the first song in the second series of *Fêtes galantes*.[39] It may be testimony to the security of their relationship that he could thus invoke a song which depicts a sculpture – a terracotta faun – laughing on the lawn as if 'predicting a bad outcome to these serene moments'. In this case, the 'bad outcome' that soon befell Debussy's marriage to Lilly was ultimately (after Emma's divorce, in turn, from Sigismond Bardac) to prepare the way to a second, more compatible union. But this happier outcome would not be won without significant personal and financial cost.

Throughout the summer of 1904, the letters Debussy wrote to Lilly at her parents' home in Yonne mixed feeble attempts to prepare the ground ('try above all not to become bored with waiting for me, you must try and be happy there, your proud and independent character will help you I hope') and insincere affirmations of continuing affection ('stop accusing me of indifference, it is too unjust!'). But when his explicit request for a separation finally came in mid-August Lilly's response proved the opposite of rational and discreet.[40] A quick return to Paris to meet her did little to calm the waters; on 13 October 1904 she attempted suicide by shooting herself in the stomach.

Although surgical intervention saved Lilly's life, the noisy condemnation that now engulfed Debussy must have seemed like a cruel negation of the acclaim he had enjoyed after the *Pelléas* premiere. Even before the suicide attempt, he wrote to Durand of his terror of returning to the gossip of Paris, 'city of light, perhaps? but city of bores too, let us admit!' By the end of October, before leaving Dieppe for further travels with Emma, he admitted being 'furiously tormented by the press campaign Madame Debussy has deliberately summoned against me', and complained that 'it seems I cannot get divorced like everyone else'.[41]

Debussy and his second wife Emma outside their home in the Avenue du Bois de Boulogne, 1908.

Bad publicity aside, the aftermath of the affair was to be a wave of 'desertions', as he put it, by those he considered his closest friends. Longstanding companions René Peter, Pierre Louÿs and Raymond Bonheur all broke ties in sympathy with Lilly; Messager and Garden followed suit; even the friendships with Dukas and Godet chilled (although with these two the breach was temporary). Of Debussy's intimate circle, only Satie and Laloy remained firm in their affections. On receiving a first letter from the latter some months later he responded with touching warmth: 'Dear friend, be sure of my joy at finding you again; I will also attempt to find again the Claude Debussy you once knew.'[42]

The pervasive disapproval seems to have arisen in part from the misapprehension that Debussy's interest in Emma was basely financial. (For Louÿs, distaste for the liaison with 'a forty-something-year-old Jewess' was compounded by anti-Semitism.[43]) But Emma came away from her divorce with little of her husband's money. And the only way Debussy was able to meet the costs of the divorce was to sell the rights to *Pelléas*. Immediately on signing the contract with the editors and receiving his part of the fee he sent Emma a ring with a letter affirming that 'for me life did not begin until the day I met you'. Less than two months after his divorce on 5 July 1905, he had gained enough detachment from his earlier life to comment sardonically to Laloy: 'you have probably read in the papers that Madame Debussy has become Mademoiselle Lilly Texier again. That is a state she should never have left. Be in no doubt that by regaining it, she will find profit and success.'[44]

A Mature Masterpiece

Torturous as the 'press campaign' about his marital problems had been, the tumult of scandal was not the only determinant of

Debussy's public profile through these months. Indeed, the same period, after the first restaging of *Pelléas* had begun in October 1903, saw the first growth of a partisan adulation for his music that would lead one critic to coin the derisive label '*Pelléastres*' for the acolytes of what was starting to seem like 'a new religion'.[45] Meanwhile, the *Prélude à l'après-midi d'un faune* was performed again both in Paris and Amsterdam; a concert in early 1904 at the salon of the Princesse de Cystria (whose *Heures de musique* were dedicated to 'the most refined, the most pure and the most delicate' music) featured several piano works, songs and the string quartet. About year later, the Salle Aeolian presented a concert featuring Debussy's string quartet together with Ravel's; recent piano music by both composers was performed by their mutual collaborator, the Catalan pianist Ricardo Viñes.

Revivals and restagings aside, it is striking just how much new work Debussy managed to produce even as he negotiated this great change in his life. Two of the piano pieces Viñes played in February 1905, *Masques* and *L'Isle joyeuse*, were newly completed; a third, *D'un cahier d'esquisses*, was finished and published with a dedication to Emma's son Raoul Bardac. The same year also saw the completion of the *Danse sacrée et Danse profane* for harp and orchestra, which (along with the incidental music for the *Chansons de Bilitis*) represent an extreme in the oeuvre of hieratic 'classical' innocence. But by far the most significant accomplishment of this period was Debussy's most grandiose triptych so far, *La Mer* – the work based on 'memories of the sea' first announced to Messager back in 1903 – whose orchestration preoccupied him all through the last months of his first marriage before it was finally finished in March 1905.

Critics inclined to hear music as composer's autobiography have been unable to resist linking some of these works directly to Debussy's personal life. Given both its title and its radiant virtuosity, for example, the piano piece *L'Isle joyeuse* ('Joyous Isle') has been readily deemed a quasi-programmatic emanation from the romantic flight with Emma to the island of Jersey.[46] A trace of that romantic seaside sojourn has even been sensed in the new, sweepingly affirmative orchestral tones of *La Mer*. No doubt such conceits now seem irredeemably crude. But there may be some value in considering this work as a crucial marker in Debussy's compositional life, at least – even as a grand affirmation in aesthetic terms of the maturity that had proved so elusive to Golaud. Whether or not it is coincidental that this affirmation emerged just as Debussy was turning from the 'woman-child character' he had first married to a more mature companion, the crucial point concerns the extraordinarily deft synthesis of contrasting elements he accomplished in *La Mer*.

The work's 'cyclic' unity, for one thing, is projected much more blatantly than in the skein of subtle thematic interconnections that link the *Trois Nocturnes*. This is not the only way in which *La Mer* seems to glance back to the Franckian models of Debussy's string quartet – indeed one fulsomely Romantic theme can be heard as a distinctly reminiscent of Franck's piano quintet, which Debussy had once admired.[47] As if to reflect the Teutonic undercurrents of the subtitle 'Three Symphonic Sketches', furthermore, the overall trajectory comes across as markedly more traditional than the previous orchestral triptych – especially in the rhetorical shapes of the first and third movements, whose powerfully affirmative perorations contrast starkly with the 'fades to silence' that end all three *Nocturnes*.

At the same time, *La Mer* marks a significant step forward in Debussy's orchestral thinking. From the start, the new prominence of the bass instruments creates a weightier, more sinewy context for the characteristic (but newly prolific) flickers of wind arabesques. Overall, the instrumentation offers countless instances of the gap between Debussy's critical posturing and his compositional imagination. In his first fictive 'interview with Monsieur Croche' (published July 1901) he had described Wagner's orchestration as 'a kind of multicoloured putty, spread almost uniformly, within which it is no longer possible to distinguish the sound of a violin from that of a trombone'.[48] Unfair as this description may be, it can serve to highlight the degree to which the *Prélude*, the *Nocturnes* and *Pelléas* had trafficked in the pure tones of single instruments. Now, in *La Mer*, the same clear hues are joined by a rich new range of orchestral 'doublings' and aqueous layering effects, through which, for example, one early theme in four horns sounds three times as if suspended in the middle depths before it fades from the scene.

Traditional resonances and orchestral detail aside, finally, it is its unfettered, improvisatory formal unfolding that was to render *La Mer* iconic for later modernists. In a book written for Debussy's 1962 centenary, for example, the composer Jean Barraqué suggested that the work seems to 'propel itself in a sense all on its own, without the aid of any pre-established model', and that 'music here becomes a mysterious and secret world that invents itself from within and destroys itself in turn'.[49] This description seems particularly apt to the second movement, 'Games of the Waves', in which the orchestra sounds at times like a loose corporation of diverse entities, free to play at their own whim, occasionally whirled together – as if by a larger, tidal force – into unitary swells. But while Barraqué may be right to celebrate the degree to which this formal unfolding seems to match the quicksilver 'linkages and superpositions' of thought itself, he underplays the degree to which the same movement's 'games' remain shot through with anthropomorphic and cultural echoes – for example in the mocking laughter scattered throughout, or the infectious waltz rhythm that drives the whole, expansive melodic excursion at the close. Here, as in the work's grand brass chorales, Debussy's 'pictorial' effects are projected through musical tropes with strong historical pedigree.

On the whole, the critical responses to the premiere at the Concerts Lamoureux in October 1905 tended, like Barraqué, to emphasize the radical aspects of *La Mer* over its myriad partly dissolved traces of tradition. The critic for *Gil blas*, for which Debussy himself had written articles in the first six months of 1903, was able to note 'some concession to symphonic development' and a few conventional phrases 'lost in the orchestral foam'. But he was more taken with the impression that '[Debussy] doesn't actually write. He is Aeolus, who breathes across an immense harp that is the orchestra.'[50] Laloy was even more extravagant, praising *La Mer* in his recently launched journal *Le Mercure musical* as 'amongst the most beautiful, the most harmonious, the most enchanting, and at the same time the broadest and most powerful [works] not only of music, but of all art, and I would almost say of nature'.[51] Laloy's fellow-editor Jean Marnold, once so dismissive of programmatic response to the *Nocturnes*, now indulged in anthropomorphisms even more extravagant than the composer's own:

> The [sea] from which the poet took inspiration this time awakens in the splendour of a sunlit dawn, beneath the plaintive caress of the wind that rocked its sleep, that watches over it, that coddles it with an egotistical and jealous love. It stretches lazily, then capriciously, and soon infuriated by the obstinate pursuit, resists, froths and bleats within the embrace, only to surrender finally, panting, in the golden brazier of noon, even as its conqueror loses strength and a chorale, surging forth from the limpid depths, celebrates their eternal marriage.

Taking issue with those who had criticized Debussy for lack of force, Marnold praised the mixture of the 'grandiose' and the 'exquisite' in *La Mer*, a music 'in which one would believe oneself to be skirting vast abysses and staring into the depths of space'.[52]

Not everyone was so convinced. The composer Alfred Bruneau, for whom *La Mer* lacked some of the 'irresistible seduction' of the *Nocturnes*, was not the only one to note a change of tone, characterized by Gaston Carraud as something 'more precise, less enveloped' than in Debussy's earlier works.[53] But it was Pierre Lalo's criticism in *Le Temps* that most annoyed the composer:

> For the first time, while listening to a picturesque work by Debussy, I have the impression of being not really in front of nature, but in front of a reproduction of nature; a reproduction that is marvellously refined, ingenious, and industrious (perhaps too much so); but a reproduction nonetheless . . . I do not hear, I do not see, I do not feel the sea.[54]

Debussy's reply took particular issue with Lalo's casual invocation of 'picturesque' motivations. Suggesting that this was a term generally used with little precise meaning, he defended the radical nature of his work:

> You love and defend traditions that no longer exist for me, or at least, they only exist as representatives of an epoch in which they were not always either as beautiful or as valuable as one might wish to maintain, and the dust of the Past is not always respectable.[55]

In this way Debussy, too, significantly exaggerated the degree to which he had shaken off the 'dust of the Past'. A full appreciation of the 'Symphonic Sketches' requires a more judicious appreciation of those aspects of its tone and language that are 'less new', as Carraud aptly put it – which is to say, its synthesis of all the most influential traditions behind Debussy's orchestral imagination.

Fatherhood, Further Projects and a Debut

The public unveiling of *La Mer* aside, the month of October 1905 also proved pivotal for more personal reasons. Only days before

Debussy and his daughter Claude-Emma, known as 'Chouchou', in 1907, Avenue du Bois de Boulogne.

the premiere Debussy moved with Emma into a *hôtel particulier* on the Avenue du Bois de Boulogne in the fashionable sixteenth arrondissement, where they would remain, beset by financial worries, until his death. On 30 October Emma bore them a daughter, Claude-Emma, known as Chouchou. Writing to Laloy in early November, Debussy both thanked him for his review of *La Mer* and gave him the news: 'I have been, for a few days, the father of a little girl – the joy of which has somewhat knocked me over and leaves me a bit fearful.'[56]

A day after Chouchou's birth, the first fruits of Debussy's 1903 vision for a series of works for piano and 'two pianos or orchestra' appeared with the publication of the first three *Images* for solo piano. It is clear from a letter to his editor that this set represented a looser kind of triptych than the *Chansons de Bilitis* or *La Mer*. But it is also clear that Debussy recognized its significance as a further step beyond the *Estampes* in his writing for piano. 'Have you played the *Images*?', he asked Durand. 'Without false vanity I believe that these three pieces will hold up well and that they will take their place in the literature for piano . . . (as Chevillard might say) to the left of Schumann or to the right of Chopin . . . as you like it.'[57] Whatever he meant by this gnomic turn of phrase, the *Images* can be said to raise the aesthetic stakes in turning from the postcard-like exoticism of the *Estampes* (about which he once quipped 'when one cannot afford to pay for travels, it is necessary to supplement with the imagination') to deeper subtexts more akin to the exploration of traditions in *La Mer*.[58] The first of the three, *Reflets dans l'eau*, though superficially an exercise in fluid pictorialism, carries palpably Romantic echoes in its climactic irruption that suggest more than one meaning of 'reflection' is in play. Historical retrospection is more blatantly at issue in the second, *Hommage à Rameau*, a grandly expressive pianistic equivalent to Debussy's critical polemics in honour of a great French precursor.

In the second instalment of this large project – a second set of three solo piano *Images*, completed a couple of years later – Debussy was to deepen and refract this pianistic engagement with time, tradition and pictorial evocation. But in the interim, he entered a relatively fallow period similar to that experienced ten years before. Throughout 1906–7, the slow gestation of several existing projects was accompanied by lengthy fruitless exchanges about new plans with potential collaborators.

The most important new interlocutor (measured by time spent if not by results) was the young writer and doctor Victor Segalen, whose published articles on contemporary aesthetics were known to Debussy, and who presented himself in April 1906 in hopes of securing his collaboration on a musical drama on the life of Buddha. Although Debussy felt some affinity for this earnest scholar of foreign cultures, claiming that Segalen's 1907 article 'Dead voices, Maori musics' interested him more than any other of its kind, he was soon retreating from the *Siddhartha* libretto with the excuse that 'in its existing form, I know no music capable of penetrating this abyss!'[59] Proposing instead a work based on the myth of Orpheus, he took the chance to criticize the eighteenth-century German composer Gluck, whose damnable displacement of Rameau in French musical affections was a recurring theme in his criticism. Gluck's opera *Orphée*, he suggested, 'had only represented the anecdotal and sentimental side of [the myth], completely neglecting everything that made Orpheus the first and most sublime of the misunderstood'.[60] But in spite of this hint at the allegorical investments behind Debussy's dramatic affinities – similarly, in explanation for his attraction to Poe's tale of the Devil he once suggested that this character 'breathes through those who do not think in the same way as everyone else' – the Orpheus project was to remain incomplete by the time Segalen's departure for China in 1909 ended their collaboration.[61]

According to Laloy, whose important early biography of Debussy was to appear in 1909, he had embarked on these labours in full expectation that they would never bear fruit. But Segalen, like Louÿs in the mid-1890s, was not the only one to find that collaboration with the composer promised more than it delivered. Exactly at the time Debussy was envisioning ways to correct Gluck's Orpheus he imagined outdoing a more recent German musical invader on the more invested terrain of the Tristan story, whose 'legendary character', he claimed, had been deformed by Wagner's 'questionable metaphysics'.[62] But while his collaboration on *The Story of Tristan* with a renewed acquaintance, Gabriel Mourey, briefly seemed promising enough to receive an anticipatory announcement in the press, a combination of practical problems and aesthetic hesitations left this project in an even less advanced state than *Siddhartha* or *Orphée-Roi*.

Clearly, the compositional impasses during these years cannot wholly be explained with reference to the vagaries of collaboration. A second Poe opera, *The House of Usher*, on which Debussy worked independently from mid-1908 through the remaining decade of his life, would also remain unfinished. All such abortive ventures aside, the paucity of new publications in these years can be put down in part to the steady progress he was making on his capacious *Images* project, whose orchestral component was ultimately to include no less than five substantial pieces. Although the sheer size of the whole collection would ultimately delay its first performance until 1913, Debussy was able to announce the completion of one orchestral *Image* (*Rondes de Printemps*) around the same time as he sent his editor the second of three sets for piano in late 1907; he claimed to Emma that a second (*Ibéria* – itself a triptych) was complete by Christmas 1908. Meanwhile, the same year saw the revision and orchestration, by Debussy alone and with younger collaborators Henri Busser and André Caplet, of several earlier works, including *L'Enfant prodigue*, *Printemps*, the two-piano *Petite suite* (of 1889), and *Le Jet d'eau* from the Baudelaire songs.

While some critics received this mining of the back catalogue – and indeed this farming out of creative labour by a renowned orchestrator – as evidence of fading revolutionary cachet, such a revival of youthful accomplishments clearly reflects Debussy's prominence and marketability after *Pelléas* and *La Mer*.[63] Indeed, relatively thin in publications though they may have been, these years saw considerable growth in his international stature, as evidenced by the productions of his opera in major European cities and beyond. Shortly after *Pelléas* received its fiftieth performance at the Opéra Comique in Paris on 23 December 1906, Debussy travelled to Brussels to observe (in exasperation) the rehearsals for the first Belgian production in January 1907. A German version was first produced in Frankfurt in April 1907 and then Munich in October 1908. In the interim, productions were mounted further afield: in New York in February 1908; in Milan in April under Toscanini (who sent a congratulatory telegram); then finally in Prague in September.

Back in Paris, the plans to present *La Mer* on the city's other significant symphony series, the Concerts Colonne, initially foundered in 'lamentable rehearsals' (as Debussy put it), which led the conductor, Édouard Colonne, to pass the baton to the composer himself. 'It is not without a strongly beating heart that I climbed the podium for the first rehearsal', he confessed to Segalen, candidly admitting his inexperience at this most public and demanding musical role. But he was also quick to celebrate a new wealth of sensations. As a conductor, he enthused, 'you truly feel at the heart of your own music . . . when it "sounds" very well, it seems as if you have become, yourself, an instrument possessing a total range of sonorities, unleashed solely at the whim of the gestures of a little stick'.[64]

By all accounts, his début with the 'little stick' was a roaring success. Noting with amusement the public's keen desire (after *Pelléas*) to glimpse the head of the '*monsieur* who wrote that', the critic 'L'Ouvreuse' vividly described the tumult that greeted the performance of the new work in the revealed presence of this 'slightly chubby paleness, ink black hair, and bulging forehead filled with ninth chords':

> The last note of *La Mer* unleashed one of those ovations that – aside from anything else – victoriously prove the solidity of a theatre and the genius of its architect . . . It lasted a duration improbable to specify, it featured cries of savage joy, clatterings of obsessed palms, demented shouts and calls. Debussy passed ten times through the forest of music stands to take the prompter's box as witness to his touched gratitude; from time to time a violent and energetic whistle, like a train conductor's signal for departure, restarted the triumphal convoy . . . recharging the zeal of tired biceps and smarting hands.[65]

While he undoubtedly savoured this triumph, Debussy's own reflections were drier in tone. Noting to Dukas how curious it was

Caricature of Debussy as a conductor, by R. Claude Bils, *c.* 1909.

that 'the feat of assembling sounds in the most harmonious possible way gives as an echo the cries of animals and the vociferations of aliens', he compared this first experience of conducting to that of 'an acrobat who has just succeeded with a difficult jump'.[66]

'To Translate a Refined Sensibility by Simple Means'

The success of this début cannot be taken as evidence of Debussy's natural gifts with the 'little stick'. Testimony to the contrary was to emerge a little over a year later when, at the invitation of the impresario Sir Edgar Speyer, Debussy crossed the Channel to conduct his music in London. As Sir Henry J. Wood, artistic director of the Queen's Hall Promenade Concerts, reported in his autobiography:

> The rehearsal went off smoothly enough but at the concert there was a peculiar accident. In the second of the *Nocturnes* (a movement called *Fêtes*), the time changes a good deal. To the surprise of all of us, Debussy (who, quite candidly, was not a good conductor, even of his own works) suddenly lost his head, and his beat! Realizing what he had done, he evidently felt the best thing was to stop and begin the movement over again. He tapped the desk, and tapped again. But then something extraordinary happened. *The orchestra refused to stop.*[67]

As it turned out, the determination of the ensemble to ignore their unreliable leader resulted in a performance successful enough to be enthusiastically encored. As Wood dryly recalled, 'Debussy was non-plussed and certainly did not understand the English mind.' An even more damning assessment of Debussy's conducting abilities was soon to emerge closer to home following the 9 April 1909 concert at the Concerts Colonne on which he presented both his early cantata *La Damoiselle élue* and a new work of 1908, the *Trois Chansons de Charles d'Orléans* for four-voice choir. This time, 'L'Ouvreuse' was distinctly ungenerous:

> It would not be a bad thing if he learned to conduct properly, because Friday, he led his four-part songs and his *Damoiselle élue* depressingly badly. Alas! yes, *mesdames*, with a feeble and timid arm, the young master shredded the gracious score that had once scandalized the Institute, and made of it a grey, somnolent, interminable affair.

While the critic was willing to blame the loss of revolutionary freshness in the cantata on Debussy's amateurish directing, he registered a more fundamental disappointment with the choral songs: 'After such a long silence, we had the right to hope for more significant discoveries from such a musician.'[68]

This response is easy to understand in view of the humble charms of the *Trois Chansons* – a strikingly unprepossessing musical reading to emerge late in the same decade that had seen the premières of *Pelléas* and *La Mer*. As in the *Trois Chansons de France* for voice a nd piano of 1904, the light tone of the selected Renaissance poems again inspired a marked simplicity of musical utterance – indeed the most traditional musical medium (SATB choir) drew from Debussy something close to the 'gracious' intertwining lyricism he had long celebrated in the music of Palestrina and Bach. The second, most recently composed song, 'Quand j'ai ouy le tabourin', is the most inventive of the three: this cosily amusing text about the poet's wish to remain warm in bed while others enjoy May time celebrations is given to a contralto solo accompanied by a tambourine-like vocal 'jangle' for all other altos, tenors and basses.

It may be, as 'L'Ouvreuse' noted, that such 'precious effects' would have been well within reach of many a more mediocre composer. But rather than any reflexive critique about a failure of imaginative scope on the part of this notorious 'Impressionist' (the label was now well established), a more generous response might take the *Trois Chansons* as evidence of a different kind of aesthetic broadening on Debussy's part, to include alongside the range of traditions absorbed and transformed in *La Mer* such humbler, 'occasional' exercises of musical craft as could be accessible to most community and church choirs. Here again, Palestrina and Bach are relevant points of reference – but in a historical sense that precedes their anachronistic canonization as exemplary pre-Romantic geniuses. A similar broadening in the direction of humility and simplicity, in fact, can be seen in the contrast between two other significant compositions Debussy managed to see into print in 1908.

The second set of piano *Images*, published in January, includes some of the most sonorously and psychologically suggestive of Debussy's creations for the instrument. Although he never suggested a specific inspiration for the first, *Les cloches à travers les feuilles* (Bells through the leaves), it is tempting to sense in the title and the deft, translucent layerings of rhythmic figures an oblique reminiscence of an idyllic report sent to Louÿs back in 1901 from a sojourn in the countryside around Lilly's parental home in Yonne. 'At that moment, the Angelus, with the voice of a little faithful – even stupid – bell was commanding the fields to sleep,' Debussy wrote, 'I found it the occasion of rhythmic combinations of which the details would make a tambourine tremble.'[69] If this piece might thus be heard to embody a kind of idealized nostalgia for rural simplicity, the second, *Et la lune descend sur le temple qui fût* (And the moon descends over the temple that was), clearly enacts, through flexible rhythmic fluctuations, a melancholy reflection on the fading promise of various 'exotic' instrumental and vocal invocations. *Poissons d'or* ('Goldfish'), finally, brings the set to a close with an acrobatic *summa* of Debussyan virtuosity, inspired by a Japanese lacquer nd dedicated to his favoured interpreter Viñes.

In marked contrast to the scope and difficulty of these *Images*, the other work Debussy completed for the piano in 1908, the six pieces of *Children's Corner* dedicated 'To my dear little Chouchou with the tender excuses of her father for that which follows', might be seen as a belated response to the 'childhood' songs of Musorgsky, *The Nursery*, he had so praised in 1901. The suggestion is more contentious than it might seem. A little while earlier, Laloy's ringing praise for Ravel's *Histoires naturelles* as a song set that both captured and transcended the 'spirit of *The Nursery*' had drawn heated objections from Debussy, who complained of Ravel's 'artificial' qualities as a 'conjuror' or 'Fakir' whose tricks could never surprise more than once.[70] (The cordial relations between the two composers largely ceased around this time, in part due to what Laloy termed 'absurd questions of priority'.[71]) While it is impossible to argue decisively for the greater 'sincerity' of Debussy's own venture into music of childhood, these little pieces remain striking for the elegance and efficiency with which they manage to 'translate a refined sensibility by simple means' (to recall his Mussorgsky review).

The 'simplicity' is far from infantile in a technical sense. The occasionally fleet finger work and pervasive subtle shadings place this music beyond the reach even of many children older than Chouchou (who turned three in 1908). Still, the way the opening piece, 'Doctor Gradus ad Parnassum', captures the learning pianist's wayward drift from earnest finger exercises into playful improvisation bespeaks a fine imaginative sympathy between mature and childish perspectives.[72] Each of the ensuing pieces demonstrates another facet of 'refinement in simplicity' – for example, in the delicate, hovering dynamism of 'The Snow is Dancing' or the miniature echo of the idyllic pastoral of 'La flûte de Pan' in 'The Little Shepherd'. But it is the last work of the set that most tellingly hints at a larger import behind the childlike pose.

In 'Golliwog's Cakewalk' a boisterous evocation of newly fashionable American dance rhythms frames a central section featuring a tongue-in-cheek quotation of the opening of *Tristan und Isolde*, marked 'with a grand emotion' and answered by a coy pianistic wink. Here, the Wagnerian 'trumpets of fame' finally seem cut down to size – reduced to an in-joke in a music-hall parody composed for a child. But it would be misleading to take this easy wit as evidence of a final resolution in this compositional relationship. Although less than a decade now remained to him, there were still further twists to come in Debussy's negotiations with all the compositional influences he had confronted to such varied ends in the years after the production of *Pelléas*. If these last years were to provide relatively few new developments on the terrain of musical reading, they were to prove rich both in the further expansion of ongoing aesthetic pursuits, and in the exploration of new compositional realms.

4

Something New, Which Surprises Even Ourselves

Not long before Debussy's death, Robert Godet – the Swiss linguist who had received, over the years, more dedicated copies of his scores than anyone else – was inspired to take a new voyage through the 'magical archipelago' of the composer's oeuvre. On disembarking from his journey of rediscovery, Godet sent his friend a letter that distils into a single colloquial phrase some of the navigational difficulties posed by the last intricate channels of this musical archipelago. 'The continuity of your effort', Godet suggested, 'is paradoxically captured in the fact that you have never drawn double profit from the same bag of grain.'[1]

As a reaction to the whole oeuvre, this observation succinctly captures the degree to which Debussy realized his own demand for all artists to 'distance themselves as much as possible from the place and subject of their success' – as he put it to a Hungarian journalist in December 1910.[2] But Godet's sense of paradoxical continuity-within-variety takes on greater weight in the face of the extreme heterogeneity of the works Debussy composed in the last eight or nine years of his life. If 1910 saw, in the first book of piano *Préludes*, a significant expansion in his facility with evocative 'masks', the next year was to find his only, disconcertingly overblown (and ostensibly sincere) work of religious music in *Le Martyre de Saint-Sébastien*. Soon after, an extreme of esotericism (*Trois Poèmes de Stéphane Mallarmé*) would share the work-table with an even sparer and simpler essay in childlike play than *Children's Corner* (the ballet

La Boîte à Joujoux). And only a year or so later, a cringingly blatant piece of wartime propaganda ('Noël pour les enfants qui n'ont pas de maison') would emerge even as Debussy was describing his last three chamber sonatas as a retreat to the haven of 'pure music'.

It would not do to over-exaggerate this last disjunction, for however remote from worldly cares the sonatas may seem the signature on their title page – '*Claude Debussy, Musicien Français*' – attaches them to the nationalism that stands behind this whole varied output as a consistent *prise de position* in these years. But Debussy's nationalistic posturing, repeated ad nauseam in letters and criticism alike, also has its ambiguities. It is unclear, for a start, just how much his list of 'French' attributes – 'clarity', 'elegance', 'charm' – really tells us about the complex formal and expressive imagination at work in many mature compositions. Furthermore, while the war years would stimulate more than one outburst of xenophobia amidst the railings against French music's enthralment to foreign influences, Debussy's writings on Wagner (to mention one contested name) actually remained more nuanced than many others. The specific problem of Teutonic influence aside, there may even be grounds – in his repeated praise for a Hungarian cafe violinist; his judicious evaluations of modern Spanish adoptions of folk music; and his exhortation to Igor Stravinsky to be 'above all, a Russian artist' – to attribute to him a more pluralistic, Herderian nationalism than is implied by those wartime pronouncements alone.[3]

On the whole, both the variegated profile of the late oeuvre and the instability of its informing ideology might seem easy to explain in light of external events – amongst which the cataclysm of the First World War was of course pre-eminent. As Debussy put it to his close friend André Caplet in 1914: 'with or without patriotism, war is an accumulation of disorder. I have a horror of disorder; thus, I do not like war.'[4] But whatever relationship might be adduced between Europe's collapse into violent chaos and the startling shifts in Debussy's later oeuvre there were other causes in place, closer to home, long before 1914. After his divorce from Lilly Debussy never gained secure financial footing. Even when supplemented by Emma's alimony from Sigismond Bardac, his earnings never came close to supporting their house in the Avenue du Bois de Boulogne along with sundry other expenses. Without the many loans – or 'advances' for work never completed – from the publisher Jacques Durand it is hard to see how the family would have survived. Given that some later projects were primarily taken up for financial reasons, it is hardly surprising that a whiff of dutiful blandness occasionally emerges.

But such instances are remarkably rare in view of the straitened circumstances of the life, which ultimately extended to an excruciating terminal illness. It would thus be misleading to overemphasize Godet's sense of paradox at the expense of an appreciation for the wealth of disparate accomplishment that emerged from several short spans of intense productivity before Debussy succumbed to cancer in early 1918. A chronological 'voyage' through the late works perhaps exaggerates discontinuities better appreciated, from a bird's eye view, as evidence of new deftness in pivoting – like one of the 'notorious dancers' who came to play a key role in Debussy's creative life – from one avenue of exploration onto another. If any one of these paths seems a new and regrettable departure, others can be seen as richly unpredictable extensions of long-developing interests. On completing his latest steps along these established lines of inquiry it is not hard to imagine Debussy sensing again the thrill he celebrated to that Hungarian journalist in 1910: 'what joy in finding within us something new, which surprises even ourselves, and fills us with calm satisfaction.'[5]

A Year of Abundance

Debussy had good cause for satisfaction by the end of a year which had proven, in spite of considerable distraction, one of his most productive. In the early months of 1910 he completed several instrumental works: the *Première Rapsodie* for clarinet; the first book of piano *Préludes*; two orchestral *Images*. A few months later, he turned again to literary-musical reading. He brought two further settings of Tristan L'Hermite's seventeenth-century verse together with 'La Grotte' from the 1904 *Trois Chansons de France* to form a new, unified triptych, *Le promenoir des deux amants*. Then he reached further back, to the Renaissance poet François Villon, for a triptych whose value in his own estimation can be deduced from the fact that these were the only songs, aside from a single Baudelaire setting ('Le Jet d'eau'), for which he completed an orchestral version.

The instrumental works completed between January and April already present a varied spectrum of accomplishment. The *Première Rapsodie*, written as a test piece for the clarinet competition at the Paris Conservatoire, is generally catalogued with Debussy's small corpus of chamber music. But it is clear from the contract that an orchestral conception was in view from the start. From a hearing of the orchestrated version (completed late 1911) it is striking how blithely the rhapsody traffics in specific echoes of the *Prélude à l'après-midi d'un faune* – a work of similar scale whose 'rhapsodic' form had been led by a different solo wind instrument. Such echoes only highlight the aesthetic distance between the two works. Not only is the relationship between solo 'figure' and orchestral 'ground' now more stable, but the rhapsody's flexible chain of improvisatory episodes actually delivers the strongest reminiscence of the *Prélude*'s agonistic lyrical effusions late in the form, as a fully satisfying moment of expressive release.

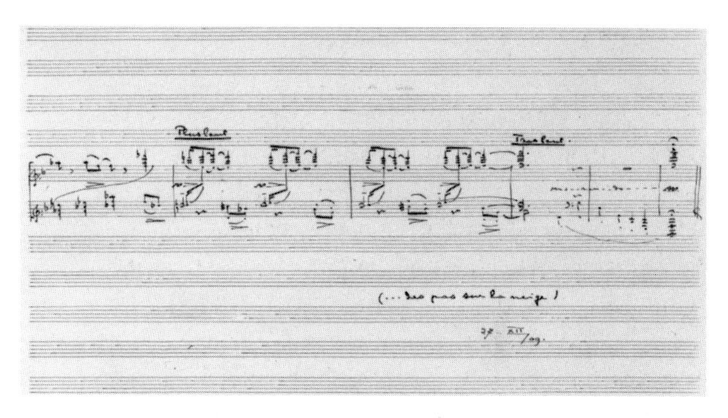

The last page of 'Des pas sur la neige' (1909), showing one of the parenthetical 'after-titles' Debussy used for all of his piano preludes.

Such slackening of allegorical investment can readily be put down to the official occasion of this 'most amiable' work (as Debussy once called it).[6] But it may also have something to do with the absence of any invested 'reading' behind the *Rapsodie*. The point might seem clearer once we note that Debussy was, at the same time, further developing the relationship between reading and composing in the first book of twelve preludes for piano. Although only a few can be tied to specific literary sources – including Shakespeare's *As You Like It* (the eleventh prelude, *La Danse de Puck*) and Baudelaire's 'Harmonie du Soir' (the fourth, *Les sons et les parfums tournent dans l'air du soir*) – Debussy structured the manuscript to encourage a new, quizzical perspective on the relationship between notated sounds and their evocative implications. Previously, he had given each *Estampe* and *Image* a conventional title atop the first page. But he now identified each prelude with a numeral, and only provided an informing poetic conceit as an elliptical afterthought below the last page.

Many of these appended hints to the performer imply modes of physical activity: dancing; turning; guitar strumming; plodding (the sixth prelude, *Des pas sur la neige*); drumming (the twelfth, *Minstrels*). The elliptical 'after-titles' thus can be read as invitations to reflect about the choreographic – tactile and gestural – experiences summoned when Debussy's modern scalar languages are deployed with evocative intent across the familiar field of the piano keyboard. The challenge, in other words, is to consider consciously the most esoteric aspects of musical experience Debussy had adumbrated, back in 1901, in his review of Dukas's piano sonata for *La Revue blanche*:

> True music lovers rarely go to fairground booths; they have their simple piano and passionately play certain pages again and again; this is just as certain a method of intoxication as the 'true, powerful and subtle opium' and a much less debilitating way of evoking happy moments.[7]

To approach some of the preludes with attunement to the combined tactile, gestural, sonorous and imaginative components of such private 'intoxication' is potentially to sense – say, within the second prelude, *Voiles*, which fleetingly releases one of Debussy's most radiant visions of 'exotic' pleasures – a further extension of the agonistic concern with expressive means and ends he had first refined years before in consultation with Mallarmé.[8]

Of course Debussy exaggerated in his description of 'true music lovers': he was to perform several of his piano preludes in public and would be closely attentive to the interpretations of others. If the first book of preludes might thus be best understood as an exploration of the boundaries between private and public musical experience rather than an endorsement of either side, Debussy was also, in early 1910, adding the finishing touches to works whose medium destined them more decisively for the 'fairground' of the public concert. The second of the three orchestral *Images*, *Ibéria*, was conducted by Gabriel Pierné at the concerts Colonne in late February 1910. A week later, Debussy directed the third *Image*, *Rondes de Printemps*, at a new concert series founded by the publisher Durand.

Although both Laloy and Ravel greeted the *Images* as further attainments of a consummate orchestral imagination, this triptych (the first piece, *Gigues*, was completed in 1913) was destined, as Boulez noted years later, to remain an 'underestimated' contribution to Debussy's orchestral oeuvre. In his attempt at a defence, Boulez tried to downplay the unifying conceit by which the triptych presents the musical 'colours' of three different countries: Scotland, Spain and France.[9] But while the elastic treatment of timbral resources partly justifies Boulez's focus on 'purely musical' aspects, Debussy gave startlingly literal emphasis after one rehearsal to precise representational qualities: 'a water-melon seller, and whistling urchins . . . I see it all quite clearly.'[10] This absurdly specific claim implicitly raises a question about whether the *Images* carry any deeper, subtextual implications along the lines of those discernible in other orchestral works. Recalling Debussy's flippant remark about the similarly folkloric *Estampes* – 'when one cannot afford to pay for travels . . . ' – the relative neglect of the *Images* within Debussyan historiography might be partly attributed to their simpler, 'postcard' level of musical evocation by comparison with the *Prélude*, the *Nocturnes* or *La Mer*.

In the two song triptychs written later the same year, on the other hand, some sort of narrative or dramatic orientation becomes explicit. First, when Debussy returned to Tristan l'Hermite to complete a triptych, *Le promenoir des deux amants*, which included one song ('La Grotte') previously presented in the *Trois Chansons de France*, he belatedly brought this poet under the unified conception of the 'song cycle' previously exemplified in triptychs on Verlaine and Louÿs. To be precise, in this case he restored the unitary conception of the source. Like Rossetti's *Blessed Damozel* l'Hermite's *Le promenoir des deux amants* is in fact a single long poem, in 28 stanzas, from which Debussy extracted three little poems for his triptych.

Although the triptych presents the nine stanzas of the three new 'poems' in l'Hermite's original order, Debussy's selection transforms the overall effect. In the original, some lengthy conventional pastoral scene-setting precedes the invitation from one lover to another to sit by a fountain; more florid verbal business then sets up their first physical intimacy – he drinks from her hands – before the poem ends with passionate embraces: 'this kiss intoxicates me, / This other one completely paralyzes me.' In Debussy's setting, the dripping languor of the first song ('La Grotte') briefly sets the scene before the second jumps ahead to the moment by the fountain ('Crois mon conseil, chère Climène'). The blithely innocent invitation that opens this central song leads, over rippling pianistic evocations of the 'sighing Zephyr', to a powerful surge of suppressed passion at the invocation of a 'rosy complexion' before it ends on a sensuous murmur. In the 'dreamily slow' third song, finally, a suave dance-like rhythm seems at first an equivalent of the speaker's vision of his lover's face 'floating within my desires' but later serves more subtly to intensify (like the rocking accompaniment to a lullaby) the childlike intimacy of Debussy's new ending, at the initial moment of intimate contact: 'Let me drink in the hollow of your hands / If the water does not melt their snow.'

While he retained l'Hermite's incremental intensification in intimacy, Debussy's excision of the consummating kisses rendered *Le promenoir des deux amants* another inconclusive cyclic musing on the elusive stages of intimate relationship. If we recall that his songs had long stood in some oblique relationship to his emotional life it may be tempting to seek similar subtextual resonances behind this decision to suspend the lovers' intimacies on an interrogative note. Indeed this triptych, like the *Trois Chansons de France* and the *Fêtes galantes II*, is dedicated to Emma, Debussy's 'dear little one'. But if the same dedication in 1904 had affirmed their first, passionate liaison, by 1910 the marriage was encountering severe instability. All through the year, Debussy's letters hinted at some sort of personal crisis. Although he never spelled out the cause, it seems clear (for example from a confession to feeling at once 'the need to flee, no matter where, and the fear of leaving') that it had much to do with the strains of 'family life' (as Lesure put it).[11] The clearest proof of marital strain is a letter Emma wrote to her lawyer, which agonizes over the pain it would cause her to 'separate from the one who makes me suffer so inexpressibly'.[12]

If it is thus tempting to read the dedication of *Le promenoir* as the mark of a freighted, penitent offering, the difficulty in affirming such personal subtexts becomes clear from a reminiscence of Debussy's publisher. On first hearing a private performance of the new triptych Durand expressed surprise that such 'delicious' music could be written at such a troubled time. Debussy replied: 'in times of drama, I feel at ease for composing.'[13] During his last years he often expressed bemusement at the light-spirited music he could create even in dire anguish.

Such a suggestion of compartmentalized life and art need not decisively undermine any hint of autobiographical resonances in *Le promenoir*. But taken together with the contrast between this triptych and the other one composed in the same year, it somewhat undercuts such lines of critique. In the *Trois Ballades de François Villon*, Debussy selected three of the sixteen or so ballads scattered through the multifarious *Testament* the Renaissance poet had penned in prison at the age of thirty. It may be tempting to read his first chosen text, 'Ballad of Villon to his Lover', as representative of a radically different response to marital difficulties. But it is hard to imagine him crudely associating himself with the 'poor man' who speaks this poem, whose 'disgrace' and 'misery' and desperate calls for help spring from the 'false beauty', 'treacherous charm' and 'concealed pride' belatedly recognized in his partner. In a wider view, it seems better to recognize this whole triptych as a further imaginative exercise in the adoption of masks – like the Spanish guitarist, Shakespearean fairy and night-club entertainer in the first book of piano preludes.

The implication is not that the characterizations lack force, but that it is impossible to trace any coherent autobiographical thread through the triptych. The second song sets a ballad written from the perspective of a pious woman praying to the Virgin Mary; the third is a twist of comic banter praising the world-leading 'gift of the gab' of Parisian women. Along with the vivid, madrigalesque intensities of the first song, the deftness with which Debussy deepens the hints of prurient fascination in Villon's ostensibly pious prayer and the skill of his comic timing in the witty third song (for example with the vaudevillian aside – 'have I named enough countries?') can be taken to link this triptych with Debussy the aspiring dramatist who had once envisioned a music adequate to convey 'all the distinct sensations of a character'. That such a simpler, more naïvely powerful demonstration of musical 'cross-dressing' could emerge simultaneously with the more intimate delicacies of *Le promenoir des deux amants* is further testimony to his late widening of aesthetic range.

Two Dancers, and a 'Mystery'

The end of 1910 brought yet more emotional turbulence. On 28 October Debussy's father, Manuel, died after a long illness. 'Although we had almost nothing in common,' he confessed to Caplet, 'it is a loss that strikes me more deeply each day.'[14] Painful as it was, the bereavement proved the occasion for renewed contacts with several friends estranged by his divorce from Lilly, notably including Godet, Dukas and Messager – for whom the operetta-loving Manuel, Debussy affirmed, had held an admiration close to religion.

A different, seemingly more mundane kind of disruption was to follow a month later, when Debussy left for an eighteen-day concert tour of Vienna and Budapest. Given the prior hints of estrangement from Emma, it is surprising just how longingly his written reports to her express the pain of separation:

> Of course you well know the *ennui* of being separated from one's 'other half', to be thinking of them to the point of anguish, only to end up holding nothingness in one's arms; but you are living amidst familiar things; your bed is full of the past; while I am living in a random, anonymous room, – whose past I had better not try and envision![15]

Although the trip was, on the whole, a ringing success in professional terms – and was to leave Debussy with a cherished memory of the 'gypsy violinist' Radics, heard in a Budapest café – he was destined to express similar extravagant pain on all the trips he took away from Emma in his later years.

Back in Paris, as he completed the ample harvest of 1910 Debussy was also still hard at work on his Poe opera. But he was soon to be deflected, as he put it in early 1911, from 'the capricious throats of singers' to 'the spiralling legs of notorious dancers'.[16] One such dancer, the Canadian Maud Allan, then enjoying considerable renown for her scantily clad appearances in *The Vision of Salome*, signed a contract with him in late 1910 for a ballet on a similarly sensuous Egyptian theme, eventually titled *Khamma*. The considerable fee was undoubtedly the main reason Debussy accepted this project on a plot that 'could be held in the hand of a child'.[17] After endless wrangles with Allan over everything from length to performing rights, he only extricated himself from the project some years later after passing off the orchestration to a younger contemporary. Although some later critics were to argue for the subtle musical qualities of *Khamma*, its subsequent neglect by conductors and critics alike can be taken to reflect an unmistakable sense of creative disengagement.

Contact with a second dancer, Ida Rubinstein, was to result in an even more controversial work Debussy initially described as 'much more sumptuous than the poor little Anglo-Egyptian ballet'.[18] This collaboration actually came to him directly from the original instigator of the work, the infamous Italian writer Gabriele d'Annunzio – 'adventurer, patriot, poet and hedonist *extraordinaire*' – who had fled his home in Tuscany for Paris to escape his creditors.[19] D'Annunzio had been struck by Rubinstein's androgynous beauty on seeing her dance in *Schéhérazade* during the first, 1909–10 Paris season of Diaghilev's renowned *Ballets russes*. He invited her to dance the lead in – and fund, from her considerable family wealth – an elaborately staged 'mystery' he was concocting, in blatant emulation of Wagner's *Parsifal*, from an overwrought mixture of Christian and pagan symbols.

Having gathered a pre-eminent painter (Léon Bakst), choreographer (Michel Fokine) and set designer (Armand Bour) to collaborate on *Le Martyre de Saint-Sébastien*, d'Annunzio and Rubinstein had been less successful in securing a composer. There was thus a hint of obsequious dissimulation in the letter Debussy received from d'Annunzio while still in Vienna:

> This summer, while I was at work on a 'mystery' I had long been pondering, a friend would often sing to me the most beautiful of your songs, with the inward voice you require. My growing work trembled, at times, with the same voice. But I did not dare to hope for you. Do you like my poetry? . . . I ask if you would wish to see me, and hear me speak of this work, and this dream.[20]

Debussy responded with great enthusiasm: 'How would it be possible for me not to like your poetry . . . The thought of working with you gives me, in advance, a kind of fever.'[21] Shortly after his return to Paris, he signed a contract with Gabriel Astruc, impresario of the 'Saison Lyrique' at the Théâtre du Châtelet, to provide an extensive list of incidental music, including orchestral preludes, dances and several vocal and choral pieces, for a production of *Le Martyre* in May and June of the following year.

The incidental music Debussy wrote for *Le Martyre de Saint-Sébastien*, his lengthiest single work after *Pelléas*, remains the most problematic stumbling-block for any attempt to follow the twisting paths through the later oeuvre. The work's plot, concocted as much from d'Annunzio's lurid imagination as from his research into medieval mystery plays, follows Sebastian, commander of the archers of Emesa, over five Acts or 'Mansions' as he first ('The Court of the Lilies') dances on burning coals to rescue Christian twins from martyrdom; then ('The Magic Chamber') conquers pagan sorceresses and encounters a wounded Virgin bearing the shroud of Christ. In the third Mansion, 'The Council of the False Gods', he mutely enacts the Passion before the Emperor Augustus Caesar using a broken-stringed lyre as a prop. Crucified on the same lyre for rejecting Caesar's offer of pagan godhood, he urges his own archers to fulfil his destiny by shooting him. A funeral procession at the end of the Fourth Mansion leads without break to the Fifth, where the gates of paradise open to receive his soul as a martyr and saint ('The Wounded Laurel' and 'Paradise').

In the face of such outré subject-matter, it is easy to see why some commentators have leant heavily on Debussy's few complaints – which largely concern the absurdly short time he had to compose – as support for dismissing most of the music for *Le Martyre* as hack-work. But the strange truth is that the majority of his statements about the project were extremely positive. In a pair of interviews in early 1911 he affirmed his interest in the libretto's 'mixture of intense life and Christian faith' and his admiration for the 'treasures of lyrical imagination' that made d'Annunzio so precious a collaborator.[22] Such public statements may be tinged with what we now call 'spin'. But it is harder to discredit the firsthand reports of Debussy weeping during rehearsals – or indeed the reverential tones in which he remembered those early moments of revelation when receiving the proofs a few months later. 'I am reminded of those precious instants of the first rehearsals – back in the time when we were still the masters', he wrote in August to Caplet, who had helped him with the orchestration. 'I think I can say those were my best and strongest memories.'[23]

Clearly, what followed had left more ambivalent traces. As rehearsals progressed, difficulties arose concerning everything from the dramatic weakness of the final scenes to the problems of ensemble singing in the cluttered sets. In the face of Bakst's pallid vision of paradise, Debussy once again found himself arguing with a set painter. To cap it all, six days before the performance the archbishop of Paris intervened in the press to remind all Catholics to avoid theatrical productions that might cause offence to conscience – amongst which he included this 'disfiguring' of a glorious martyr.[24] In an open letter, Debussy and d'Annunzio earnestly reaffirmed the 'profoundly religious' quality of their work.[25] Elsewhere, Debussy insisted that he had composed his music 'as if it were commissioned for a church'.[26]

From the perspective of the impresario d'Astruc such a contretemps likely came as useful publicity: by some reports, Catholics eagerly swarmed to the first performances. And in spite of all the difficulties, the press premiere of *Le Martyre de Saint-Sébastien* on 21 May 1911 was far from a critical disaster. To be sure, many balked at d'Annunzio's 'interminable' anti-dramatic monologues (as Laloy put it), whose sheer tedium over more than five hours made Debussy's 55 minutes of music seem relatively inconsequential.[27] Still, it is surprising just how warmly some critics did respond. For Gaston Carraud, the music demonstrated 'new firmness of sonority and accent'.[28] For Alfred Bruneau it even represented an important breakthrough: 'until now, Debussy's art has been instrumental above all. Here, it is principally choral and attains an entirely new force.'[29] It is strange that Bruneau could give such one-sided emphasis to the instrumental productions of a composer so long engaged with vocal arts. But he prefigured the later consensus that the greatest strengths of the music for *Le Martyre* emerge in certain

Léon Bakst, line drawing of Ida Rubinstein in the armour of Saint Sébastien, 1911; a costume-design for the 1911 theatre-piece.

choral episodes, where even one particularly harsh later critic finds Debussy approaching his 'Renaissance ideal'.[30]

However close Debussy may have come to the style of his beloved Palestrina, it is still hard to accept even the best of the choruses in *Martyre* as a full realization of the high ideals for incidental music he expressed in one of those 1911 interviews. Reaching beyond the most exacting of his youthful visions for a music that 'clothes the poetry' he now claimed to be seeking a music 'which must become one body, intimately, with the text'.[31] The phrase betrays a renewed susceptibility to Wagnerian enthusiasms like those hyperbolically expressed by d'Annunzio after a rehearsal of the last scene: 'Like Sebastian nailed to the Lyre, Music and Drama cry "*We are One!*"[32] Ironically, it is precisely the question of its pervasive debts to

Parsifal, along with the difficulty of framing any cogent response to the whole 'curious hybrid' of recitation, dance and music, that together have rendered *Le Martyre* the hardest of all Debussy's works to assimilate.[33]

More than any other work, the degree to which one is willing to be 'surprised' by Debussy seems to determine how the music for *Le Martyre* is received. Does it betray a loss of balance between compositional inclinations and limitations, which leaves a 'ramshackle' assemblage of 'imitation Wagner' whose only value is its expansion of Debussy's emotional range to include *Parsifal*'s darker realms of guilt and expiation?[34] Or if its extreme eclecticism is accepted as typical of incidental music, can the echoes of both *La Damoiselle élue* and *The Fall of the House of Usher* in *Le Martyre* be heard to render it 'a central point of reference in Debussy's theatrical career'?[35] At any rate, the initial 'mystery' was never to be restaged after its first run of nine performances. Although Debussy would continue planning revisions up to the end of his life, *Le Martyre* is now known primarily through curtailed concert adaptations prepared by the original chorus director Émile d'Ingelbrecht in 1912 and by Caplet in 1914.

Nijinsky and Stravinsky

There was to be little chance for Debussy to resume work on his Poe opera even once *Le Martyre* had been released into the world, for within a few weeks he was away to Turin on another conducting trip. Musically, this was to be one of his least satisfying journeys. The musicians seeming both ill-prepared and indifferent to his music, Debussy handed the rehearsals over to the young conductor Vittorio Gui. At least the company of Emma and Chouchou, this time, could have been expected to save Debussy from his customary pain of separation. But Emma's constant indisposition (along

Debussy at Houlgate on the Normandy seaside, 1911.

with the noise of the trams) nonetheless left him complaining that 'a trip that could have been a pleasure has become an odious nightmare!'[36]

The return to Paris, to confront belatedly the exhaustion he had been feeling after *Le Martyre*, inspired visions of more relaxing ventures. A nudge to Durand – 'in looking for the most ingenious combinations, I'm still missing three thousand francs, which, even by selling my soul to the devil, I don't know where to find!' – was enough to secure funds for a month's family vacation at Houlgate by the sea.[37] Here again Debussy found himself at odds with the joys of travel, writing wryly to Caplet about such rituals of hotel life as the need to change clothes four times a day (photos on the beach show him in his usual natty urban attire) and the 'barbarous' impositions of 'civilization' on the seaside. Quoting Pelléas's idyllic vision of 'children going down to the beach to bathe' he added a misanthropic postscript: 'But my lord! How unsightly to contemplate are *Messieurs* their papas and *Mesdames* their mamas!' His attempts to finish scoring the clarinet rhapsody and the last of the *Images* having been disrupted by the whole 'caravansary', he settled for reading cheap novels instead.[38]

Given this curmudgeonly attitude to travel it is perhaps surprising that the return to Paris was to find Debussy contemplating a much more extensive voyage, to present *Pelléas et Mélisande* in Boston. His exchanges with Caplet about this new plan betray further background tensions with Emma, who neither wished to come along nor wanted to let him go alone. Reluctantly, Debussy secured Caplet's agreement to go in his stead, pleading 'very serious familial reasons' as his excuse to the impresario Henry Russell. Denied this new involvement with his one complete opera, an attempt to revive his labours on the two Poe libretti only led to further frustrations.[39] Finding that he could still see the 'seams' in what he had completed, he scrawled in exasperation a phrase that testifies how resolutely he clung to stringent musico-dramatic ideals even after recent disappointments: 'How much it is necessary to find, and then suppress, in order to arrive at the naked flesh of emotion.'[40]

As it happened, attempts to excavate such naked emotion from beneath the dead weight of operatic traditions were to be deflected yet again by dance projects. Even as negotiations about *Khamma* sporadically continued with Maud Allan, an exchange began with the symbolist poet Charles Morice about *Crimen Amoris,* a 'sung and danced poem in the style of Verlaine', and proceeded over the first few months of 1912 to a signed publisher's contract and discussions about a production with Messager, who had been director of the Opéra since 1908. But while Debussy expressed a vivid sense of choreographic and colouristic detail in his early exchanges with

Morice and would still be discussing the project under the new title *Fêtes galantes* as late as 1914, he was never to complete any music for this balletic 'reading' of a poet who had inspired so many of his songs.

Meanwhile, another product of early literary encounters, the *Prélude à l'après-midi d'un faune*, was undergoing its own translation to the 'spiralling legs of notorious dancers' without significant input from Debussy himself. His familiarity with the dazzling productions of Diaghilev's *Ballets russes* extended back, before his involvement with Ida Rubinstein, to the company's first Parisian season in 1909–10. (At that time he had even worked briefly on a ballet scenario, *Masques et Bergamasques*, at Diaghilev's invitation.) In June 1910, having met Igor Stravinsky for the first time at the première of the ballet *The Firebird*, he had praised the music of the brilliant young Russian both for its unheard-of 'rhythmic concordances' and for being much more than a 'docile servant of dance'. His admiration for and friendship with Stravinsky subsequently grew to the point that he could send him, a year later, the highest imaginable praise for the music of *Petrouchka*, Stravinsky's second project with Diaghilev, when claiming to hear in it 'the kind of orchestral *certainties* I have not encountered since *Parsifal*'.[41]

In retrospect, there is a faint irony in Debussy's admiration for the way Stravinsky's *Firebird* music transcended simple servitude to dance. For when his own faun *Prélude* was drawn into a *Ballets russes* programme in early 1912, he was to react with horror at the disjunction between music and choreography – the very quality that earned the production epochal status in dance history. In fact, the *Prélude* had been chosen by Diaghilev to accompany a highly stylized choreographic vision his famously charismatic lead dancer (and lover) Vaslav Nijinsky had been developing through study of the postures on ancient Greek vases.[42] Nijinsky had initially found Debussy's music, though perfect in 'sentiment' and 'atmosphere', too 'hazy' and 'soft' for the new angular style of

Debussy and Igor Stravinsky in 1910, around the time the Russian composer was first gaining fame with his ballet scores *l'Oiseau de feu* and *Pétrouchka*.

movement he was exploring.[43] But Diaghilev's nose for publicity won over, and after an inordinate number of rehearsals Nijinsky's choreography of the *Prélude à l'après-midi d'un faune* was staged at the Théâtre du Châtelet, with sumptuous decor by Léon Bakst, on 29 May 1912.

It may be easy, on first viewing one of the many reconstructions of this ballet, to understand why Debussy recoiled in disgust at the 'dissonance' between his supple music and Nijinsky's 'angular' gestures.[44] But closer consideration discovers a rich interaction between the distinct layers of this 'balletic reading of a musical reading of a poem'. While some later reports would emphasize Nijinsky's indifference to the poem, both the overall scenario (a faun wakes from slumber, sees several nymphs and pursues one, then settles back to sleep after her escape) and certain visual details (the pipe he plays at the start; the grapes he raises to the sky) draw directly on Mallarmé's imagery. As for the 'dissonance' with the *Prélude*, the sensuously dappled faun and decorously draped nymphs may indeed seem to shuttle against the sonorous backdrop like 'figures of cardboard', as Debussy complained, but the dance nonetheless unfolds with some sensitivity to the music's formal outlines. Most notably the central, static but oddly intimate *pas de deux* between the faun and a single nymph begins just as Debussy starts his transition to the climactic lyricism; poignantly, their most intimate gesture (they briefly hook elbows) occurs not at the musical climax but after, once the string melody has faded to a wispy memory for solo violin.

Such subtleties were largely lost to view within the tumultuous reception of the first performance. A rousingly enthusiastic initial response, which led Diaghilev to order an immediate encore, found its opposite in the heated press censure that greeted Nijinsky's final action: lying astride a scarf dropped by his desired nymph, he had given a tiny pelvic thrust. Predictably, prudish critical outrage at this 'erotic bestiality' only served to guarantee the work a *succès de*

Vaslav Nijinsky as the faun, confronting a nymph in his 1912 ballet *Prélude à l'après-midi d'un faune*. Debussy objected to the angular choreography.

scandale, although later audiences found their prurience disappointed by the suppression of the offending gesture.[45] The planned run of four performances was extended to eight, overshadowing the two productions of *Daphnis et Chloé* choreographed by Michel Fokine to the music of Ravel that closed the 1912 season.

It is unclear whether Debussy found any satisfaction in this partial sacrifice of Ravel's ballet to Nijinsky's *Prélude,* for he made surprisingly little reference to the whole affair in his letters. But as it turned out, he was destined to suffer similar overshadowing himself once he accepted a commission to write an original score for a second Nijinsky dance. The scenario for *Jeux* (Games), as the new ballet was called, offered more up-to-date imagery than the faun's stylized archaicism:

> In a park, at twilight, a tennis ball has gone astray; a young man, then two young women eagerly look for it. The artificial light of the tall electric lamps that cast a fantastic glow all around them inspires them to childish games: they chase each other, hide from each other, quarrel and sulk without reason; the night is warm, the sky filled with glimmers, they embrace. But the charm is broken by a tennis ball thrown by some unknown malicious hand. Surprised and scared, the young man and the young women disappear into the depths of the nocturnal park.[46]

While it hardly seems more robust than the 'Anglo-Egyptian' plot he had found so flimsy, Debussy later described this scenario as the kind of 'nothing at all' that was perfectly appropriate for a 'ballet poem'. Indeed by characterizing it as 'all that is necessary to give birth to rhythm in a musical atmosphere', he casually encapsulated the two most distinctive qualities of the coruscatingly imaginative score he wrote for Nijinsky's *Jeux*, which was premièred almost exactly a year after the *Prélude*.[47]

In terms of its sonorous 'atmosphere', for a start, to evoke what he melodramatically described as the 'horrors' that take place amidst the three characters Debussy makes far subtler use of the darker expressive hues of *Parsifal* in *Jeux* than he had in *Le Martyre*.[48] He explicitly acknowledged the model in this case when writing to Caplet of his search for 'that orchestral colour that seems as if lit from behind, of which there are such marvellous examples in *Parsifal*'.[49] On the other hand, the reference in the same letter to an ideal 'orchestra without feet', while suggestive of the work's 'aerian' qualities (as one critic put it), is deceptive to the degree that it deflects attention from his clever play with dance rhythms. This aspect of *Jeux* had been emphasized by Diaghilev in his initial remit: '*Nijinsky* says that he is envisioning above all some "*dancing*". – Scherzo – waltz – a great deal of work *en pointe* for all *three*.'[50] If the impresario savoured the scandal value of a man in point shoes, for Debussy the call to write music for '*dancing*' inspired games with conventional rhythms just as brilliantly ironic as his musings on traditional lyricism had been in the *Prélude* almost two decades before.

Here again, the point has been obscured by later appropriations of Debussy's *Jeux* as the precursor of mid-century modernist ideals. But however readily it might be claimed as a model for 'quasi-statistical accumulation of sound' or 'methods of musical time . . . engendered from within the work itself' (as one influential 1959 essay put it), this mercurial score is just as significant for its subtle engagement with the musical past encapsulated in Diaghilev's reference to 'dancing – scherzo – waltz'.[51] While some trace of the *Prélude*'s concern with lost lyricism remains in the vestigial wisps of nostalgically sweet high violin sound that mark key moments of intimacy, *Jeux* is constructed more intensively around a few archetypical 'waltz' gestures that emerge from a kaleidoscopic variety of more abstract rhythmic figures. Periodically surging into prominence to support the various couplings and recouplings of the scenario, these impassioned revenants of the most iconic Romantic dance form receive their ultimate apotheosis in the music for the last, threefold embrace that precedes the ballet's crepuscular close.

When he finally saw the choreography, Debussy was understandably disappointed to find that Nijinsky had actually conceived no similar play on traditional 'dancing' but rather an aridly arithmetical concoction redolent of his studies with dance guru Émile Jaques-Dalcroze – in Debussy's opinion 'one of the worst enemies of music'. Complaining, after the premiere, about the dancer 'watching the music go by with a disdainful eye', he later defined his distaste more explicitly when recalling how the 'cruel and barbarous choreography' had 'stamped on my poor rhythms as if on a noxious weed'.[52] No doubt this choreographic 'abstraction', which made the flirtatious games seem to one critic 'as if traced on a blueprint',

Nijinsky as a tennis player in the 1913 tennis-inspired ballet *Jeux*. Debussy was again disappointed by the choreography, and the work was overshadowed by Stravinsky's *Le Sacre du Printemps*.

partly explains why *Jeux* met with little acclaim at its premiere on 15 May 1913.[53] But if the result was more a near-invisibility than a failure – as Lesure put it, 'no score went so unnoticed as *Jeux*' – a more important reason was the fact that the work had been prepared alongside a much more radical choreographic collaboration between Nijinsky and Stravinsky.[54] Beyond simply overshadowing *Jeux*, the riotous premiere of *Le Sacre du Printemps* that followed just two weeks later was to become one of the most mythologized moments in the history of modern music and dance.

Debussy was well aware of the hair-raisingly powerful music in preparation for this other ballet, for he had played a four-hand piano version with Stravinsky at Laloy's home in the summer of 1912. He later confessed to Stravinsky that the experience 'haunts me like a beautiful nightmare', leaving him 'waiting for the production like a greedy child who has been promised some sweets'.[55] But the only firsthand record we have of his response to the ballet is one comment to Caplet after the dress rehearsal: '*Le Sacre du Printemps* is something extraordinarily wild . . . If you wish: it is savage music with all of modern comforts!'[56]

While this may be a reasonable response to the *Rite*'s monumental hybrid of 'archaeological' primitivism and modernist technique, from some reports it is clear that Debussy felt some ambivalence about a ballet whose rhythmic experiments may have seemed to trample the 'scherzos' and 'waltzes' of *Jeux* even more cruelly than Nijinsky's Dalcrozian choreography. The writer Georges Jean-Aubry, for one, recalled that Debussy, while admiring the work's power, fell back on his usual nationalism to sniff that 'still, that's not the way we will make French music'.[57] There is likely some truth, furthermore, in Stravinsky's self-serving recollection that Debussy found himself unable to 'digest' the *Rite* as easily as many younger composers.[58] Indeed, he himself offered oblique support to this view when, on receiving a dedicated piano score of the *Rite* from Stravinsky some months later, he wrote in reply: 'for me who is descending the other side of the hill while still retaining an ardent passion for music, there is particular satisfaction in declaring how much you have pushed back the permissible boundaries of the empire of sounds.'[59]

Last Preludes, Last Ballet, Last Reading

It is clear from more than Jean-Aubry's testimony alone that Debussy was able to retain his lifelong intransigence even in full awareness that he was 'descending the other side of the hill'. In late 1912, even as he penned one of his most forceful polemics in favour of Rameau at Caplet's behest, he also reluctantly launched a last stint of professional criticism for the *Revue de la S. I. M.* with a jeremiad urging for music's release from 'those who profit from it while usurping the good name of artists'.[60] We might wonder how he could presume that all own labours 'for hire' transcended such suspicion. But after a year or two devoted to works of an extravagantly public nature, in mid-1913 he turned back to more esoteric pursuits.

A second book of twelve *Préludes*, first of all, represents a further stage in Debussy's pianistic explorations of the relationship between private 'intoxication' and evocative musical powers. In considering the relationship between this volume (published April 1913) and the previous one, it helps to recall Gatti's sense of the 'concentric circles' of Debussy's development.[61] For if it is possible to pair many of the preludes in the second volume with those in the first – the 'ancient Egyptian' evocation in *Canope*, for example, answers the 'Grecian' accents of *Danseuses de Delphes*; the music-hall witticism of *Général Lavine: Eccentric* descends directly from *Minstrels* – the overall progression is far from straightforward. Of the two evocations of the Celtic North, for example, the second book's *Bruyères* (Heaths) seems even more idyllically naive than the first book's ever-popular *La fille aux cheveux de lin* (Girl with the Flaxen

Hair). But of the two 'Spanish' pieces, while the first book's *La Sérénade interrompue* offered distinct pianistic pleasures in its imitations of a strumming guitar, the more violent, gesturally unfettered intensity of the second book's *La Puerto del Vino* enacts the more complex relationship between pianistic choreography and abstract musical coherence.

Gatti felicitously framed the questions now coming into focus in Debussy's pianism when he admitted to some ambivalence about what he felt as a displacement of conventional musical values by purely 'epidermic' sensations.[62] Indeed in certain preludes the quasi-improvisational gestures seem to emerge directly from the array of black and white keys on the piano, confronting the relationship between music's evocative poetry and its conventional materials in a way entirely in keeping with the legacy of Mallarméan Symbolism.[63] To sense such questions in Debussy's piano music is again to confront the larger tension between private, solipsistic experience and public communication. There is perhaps no more vivid illustration of the potential for this tension to become something approaching a contradiction than the two works for which Debussy signed a single publishing contract in July 1913.

Each marks an end to one of Debussy's paths of exploration. The ballet *La Boîte à joujoux* ('The Toybox') was to be his last work for the stage (Caplet finished the orchestration after his death). The *Trois Poèmes de Stéphane Mallarmé* was his last song triptych – indeed the last of his significant musical readings. The scenario for *La Boîte à joujoux* was adapted from an illustrated children's story by André Hellé about a love triangle between a doll, a cardboard soldier and a clown. Absurd as it may seem to note that Debussy's opera had used a similar theme, he invoked Maeterlinck in support of the idea that this little ballet might best be presented by the 'mysterious souls' of dolls or marionettes.[64] But at the same time, he found in Hellé's illustrations of the various scenes an ideal of simplicity which he expressly wished to match in music.[65] The several echoes of *Children's Corner* are only the clearest sign of Debussy's intention for this music, like the earlier collection, to serve as a paternal offering to Chouchou. The piano score Debussy published, though full of deft thematic interrelationships and parodic winks at Gounod and Mendelssohn, perfectly fulfils the goal he expressed to Durand: 'I have tried to be clear, and even "amusing" without pretension, and without useless acrobatics.'[66]

If *La Boîte à joujoux* thus brings Debussy's balletic explorations to a close on the tone of paternal warmth with which he always referred to Chouchou, the close of his career as a reader of sophisticated literature is harder to link to his life. Breaking the precedent of the *Trois Chansons de France*, the *Fêtes galantes II*, and *Le promenoir des deux amants*, the last triptych, *Trois Poèmes de Stéphane Mallarmé*, is not dedicated to Emma but 'to the memory of Stéphane Mallarmé and in respectful homage to Mme. E. Bonniot (née G. Mallarmé)'. Nearly thirty years after setting 'Apparition' Debussy thus rounded off his literary-musical explorations with a personal homage to the poet whose *L'Après-midi d'un faune* had inspired his most sophisticated musical response to poetic form. But it is hard to trace any allegorical progression through the late Mallarmé triptych, in which each chosen poem articulates a highly refractory first-person declaration to a woman. In the absence of the quasi-narrative continuity of *Le promenoir des amants*, the whole unfolds as a loose collation of musings on the theme of intimate encounter.

After he had composed his Mallarmé songs and belatedly sought permission from the poet's executor, Debussy learned of an extraordinary coincidence. Not only had Ravel also been inspired by the appearance of a new edition of Mallarmé to write a triptych of songs, but he had even selected two of the same poems. Although the Ravel triptych would not appear for another year, its juxtaposition with Debussy's last reading of Mallarmé seems in retrospect a milder version of the overshadowing *Jeux* had suffered alongside *The Rite of Spring*. The sense of disparity of accomplishment is perhaps most unavoidable in the settings of the poem both composers chose as the first song in their triptychs.

The poem, 'Soupir' (Sigh), one of Mallarmé's finest symmetrical structures, both enacts and holds in suspended solution a rich metaphorical equivalence between the striving of the speaker's soul towards the eye and brow of his 'calm sister' and a fountain perpetually rising from a melancholy pool towards the azure October sky:

> *Mon âme vers ton front où rêve, ô calme soeur,*
> *Un automne jonché de taches de rousseur,*
> *Et vers le ciel errant de ton oeil angélique*
> *Monte, comme dans un jardin mélancolique,*
> *Fidèle, un blanc jet d'eau soupire vers l'Azur!*
> *– Vers l'Azur attendri d'Octobre pâle et pur*
> *Qui mire aux grands bassins sa langueur infinie*
> *Et laisse, sur l'eau morte où la fauve agonie*
> *Des feuilles erre au vent et creuse un froid sillon,*
> *Se traîner le soleil jaune d'un long rayon.*
>
> [My soul towards your brow where dreams, o calm sister / An autumn strewn with freckles / And towards the shifting sky of your angelic eye / Climbs, as in a melancholy garden, / Faithful, a white fountain sighs towards the azure! / Towards the tender azure of a pale and pure October / Which mirrors in the great basins its infinite languor / And lets, over the dead water where the tawny agony / Of the leaves drifts in the wind and ploughs a cold furrow, / Be drawn out from the yellow sun a long ray.]

Debussy's setting shows all of the lyrical flexibility and pianistic imagination that he had developed over decades of song-writing. But in a sense, Ravel trumps his reading from the start by setting the poem to an instrumental ensemble (flute and piccolo, clarinet and bass clarinet, string quartet and piano) that responds with great subtlety to the poem's autumnal hues. One of the most inspired conceptions of a pre-eminent instrumental colourist, the song is also exceptional for the hypnotic power of its lyrical pacing. Entering low, beneath a high radiant rustle of string sound, the voice unfurls a continuous 'sigh' of melody that swoops gradually upwards as the accompaniment accumulates depth and resonance, to deliver an epiphanic arrival on '*Fidèle*' (faithful) before settling back for more darkly tinted later episodes.

Retrospective evaluations aside, in late 1913 Debussy was able to view the coincidental choice of two poems with some humour, describing it to Durand as 'a phenomenon of auto-suggestion worthy of a message to the Academy of Medicine!'[67] Unlike Ravel, who dipped into the most obscure corners of Mallarmé's art to end his triptych with the sonnet 'Surgi de la croupe et du bond', Debussy opted for a more delicate piece of occasional verse as the text of his last significant song.

'Autre éventail' (Other fan) is one of several poems Mallarmé wrote on fans as gift offerings, in this case for his daughter Geneviève. This precious little text, written as the fan's supplication to the 'dreamer' who holds it in her hand, inspired one of Debussy's most whimsical settings. A scatter of exclamatory fragments set to a spare flutter of piano figuration, it saves its most sensuous hues for a final image – 'The sceptre of rosy shores / Stagnant beneath the golden evenings' – that revisits the vespertinal close of Mallarmé's faun poem. A few faint traces of the 1894 *Prélude* can be discerned in the closing passages, but the more tellingly valedictory detail is to be heard in the last vocal utterance. Relinquishing his literary-musical explorations with a final taste of the characteristic 'singing' style long ago used for the first words of Mallarmé's 'Apparition' – and later for Bilitis's '*Ma mère ne croira jamais*' and Mélisande's '*Je t'aime aussi*' – Debussy narrows down the last melodic line to deliver the closing image, a 'white, closed flight' posed against 'the fire of a bracelet', on a single, chanting pitch.

More Travels and Frustrations

As Debussy worked on *La Boîte à joujoux* and the Mallarmé songs through the later months of 1913, he also added to his list of incomplete projects by signing a contract for another ballet, on a Chinese theme (*Le Palais de Silence*, later *No-ja-li*). In a solo flute piece written for the play *Psyche* (later published as *Syrinx*) he finished the only music to emerge from his various attempts at collaboration with Gabriel Mourey. Although the year as a whole had proven relatively productive, this was not enough to prevent him from again courting near-suicidal anguish. Once more, the problems were primarily of a material nature, compounded by the tensions these inevitably created with Emma. In part to supplement scant resources, on 1 December Debussy embarked on his longest tour abroad. At the invitation of the great conductor Serge Koussevitzky, he left for Russia for two weeks to present his music in Moscow and St Petersburg.

The telegrams sent to Emma en route testify pathetically to the pain of separation: 'All the poor love of Claude'; 'Unhappy Night. Unhappier sleeper'; 'Do not forget your Claude'; 'I am here, Alas.'[68] Once he had arrived and rehearsals were under way, he felt it necessary to remind her that he was undertaking the trip 'to serve us'. His difficulty in convincing her of this point is illustrated most clearly in a letter sent from Moscow about half way through the trip:

> You wrote 'I do not know how to prevent myself from holding some rancour about your music' . . . Do you not see how there might be something a little maddening in that? In truth,

> between you and music, if there is anyone who should be jealous, it is surely music! And, if I continue to make it and love it, it is surely because I owe to this very music you treat so badly the fact that I have known you, loved you, and all the rest![69]

As the trip continued to its second phase, not even the comforts of the Grand Hôtel d'Europe in St Petersburg were enough to give Debussy back his 'beautiful sleeps of a spoiled child'. But while insomniac yearning for Emma may have contributed to the air of suffering one Russian composer later recalled, it did not prevent him from conducting a memorable performance of *La Mer*. Acknowledging the 'strange charm' in the inexpert conducting of many composers, the same witness affirmed: 'a touching beauty is revealed through this combination of technical clumsiness and an interpretation that is both personal and convincing to the highest degree.'[70] The musicians of Koussevitzky's orchestra proved similarly forgiving of technical shortcomings when they signed a note thanking Debussy for experiences that were to remain 'like explosions of light that will forever brighten our musical career'.[71]

Back in Paris, in early February Debussy accompanied the violinist Arthur Hartmann in a concert of violin and piano arrangements of his own songs and preludes, along with the violin sonata by Edvard Grieg. While he clearly saw the arrangements as another potential source of income it is harder to account for his interest in the Grieg, whose music he had once cuttingly compared to a 'pink sweet covered in snow'.[72] But this more recent encounter seems to have inspired the more generous comparison of Grieg's music, in his last regular article for the *Revue de la S. I. M.*, with the 'icy freshness' of Norway's lakes and the 'urgent ardour' of its short springs. Amusingly, the same article criticizes a 'symphonic illustration' of a poem by the younger composer Gabriel Grovlez in terms that could equally well have been directed at his own orchestral illustration of Mallarmé many years before: 'if poetry can change its setting at will, music can not be turned around quite so easily'; 'the artifice of the explicative programme disappears . . . the mind starts to create its own personal story.'[73] While his sense of the gulf between his own readerly gifts and those of Grovlez likely masked this parallel from him, it nonetheless remains surprising, given his experiences with Nijinsky, that he could propose a 'scenic realization' as a possible solution to the problems of such an orchestral reading.

Before this article appeared on 1 March 1914, Debussy was away on more travels: to Rome in late February; then to Amsterdam and The Hague until early March. While sending the most hysterical of all his plaints to Emma from Rome – 'all night truly I had the sincere impression that I was going to die' – Debussy was able to muse more philosophically to Durand about the possibility that his distress had something to do with a sense of lost time since his residency at the Villa Medici thirty years earlier.[74] The orchestral concert on 21 February, at any rate, was a great success. And while Debussy bemoaned the 'subtle cruelty' of the brief stop in Paris before he had to leave again, the concerts in the Netherlands were similarly greeted by 'tumultuous ovations'. On returning, he was only to enjoy a scant few weeks characterized by a few scattered exchanges about various productions and rather more about financial difficulties before he was off again, to Brussels, where he played several preludes and images and accompanied the singer Ninon Villat-Pardo in *Le promenoir des deux amants* and the *Chansons de Bilitis*.

A momentary lull in his wanderings saw Debussy, through the late spring and summer of 1914, engaging with the latest offerings of Parisian musical life. D'Annunzio accompanied him and Emma to a performance of Verdi's *Otello* featuring Nellie Melba in early May; a few weeks later the couple joined society hostess Misia Edwards in her box at the Opéra for the *Ballets russes* production of Rimsky-Korsakov's *Le coq d'or* and Stravinsky's *Petrouchka*. Early

June presented an intriguing juxtaposition when, on the expiration of Bayreuth's thirty-year exclusive contract, *Parsifal* received its first Parisian staging only a day after the latest production of *Pelléas et Mélisande*. Debussy left us no response to the Verdi, the Rimsky or the Wagner, but proved as exacting as ever about his own opera. In a detailed letter of critique he warned the conductor Franz Ruhlmann, among other things, that 'the first scene of the 4th Act is taking on the pace of a gallop: one might say that Pelléas and Mélisande are afraid of missing their train.'[75] This was to be the last Parisian production of *Pelléas* in his lifetime.

Although consultations continued with Hellé on *La Boîte à joujoux* and with d'Annunzio on a film version of *Le Martyre* and a new 'Indian drama', the only new composition in the first half of 1914 was a suite for two pianos, *Six Épigraphes Antiques*, partly adapted from the incidental music written years earlier for the recitation of the *Chansons de Bilitis*.[76] When writing to Godet of his dissatisfaction with this paucity of accomplishment Debussy again touched that extreme of fatalism that had regularly recurred since the mid-1890s:

> For four and a half months, I have been able to do exactly nothing! Naturally, such things lead to miserable domestic spats and to hours during which one can hardly perceive any other way out except for suicide . . . Ah! the 'magician' who you loved in me, where is he? This one is now no more than a gloomy mountebank who will soon break his back in an ultimate pirouette bereft of all beauty.[77]

But such dire personal predictions were to be overshadowed by the unimaginably more serious crisis that soon befell all of Europe. By the time Debussy returned in late July from one further trip to perform with the tenor Enrico Caruso in London the assassination in Sarajevo had precipitated the initial declarations of war. In early August, he admitted to Durand how useless it seemed to speak further about his private concerns in view of the far grander problems inevitably in store.

Debussy and the War

Debussy's initial response to the war was a contradictory blend of candour at his own lack of 'military spirit'; worry about Emma's son and son-in-law (both of whom were in the army); and envy of his friend Satie for participating with a socialist militia in the defence of Paris.[78] Within a couple of weeks a more distasteful note typical of the mental reflexes so often triggered in wartime crept in. Using a racist term of abuse – *métèques* – best translated as 'dagoes' or 'wogs', Debussy wrote approvingly to Durand about the government's evacuation and internment of foreigners: 'Since they cleansed Paris of all of its *métèques*, whether by shooting them or by throwing them out, it has immediately become a charming place. And truly one only encounters no more than a minimum of ugly mugs!'[79]

The casual cruelty may be hard to swallow, but the underlying racist susceptibility should hardly come as a surprise. Debussy was just as ready as most of his generation to use a term like 'negro' in a derogatory sense (for example when noting the simple-mindedness of Maud Allan's scenario for *Khamma*). Still, it is hard not to sense a bizarre contradiction between what we might call the 'multicultural' musical spectrum – Far Eastern, Slavic, African-American – he had long drawn on for inspiration, and this wartime question to Durand: 'did not our supposed [national] decay arise from that wave of foreigners who flooded Paris with a whole variety of horrors, finding the opportunity to accomplish them here more freely than in their own country?' In hindsight, perhaps 'contradiction' is too mild a word for such a conflation of aesthetic and moral concerns, given its kinship with the ideology that would, twenty-odd years later, seek the elimination not only of 'decadent art' but also 'sub-human people' through similar appeals to racial purity as in Debussy's next assertion: 'the French soul will remain forever clear and heroic.'[80]

Still, if the line linking Debussy's wartime chauvinism to the most vicious later forms of nationalist ideology seems less than clear, that is because the primary target of his repugnance was not any unfortunate 'foreign worker' but rather the *esprit bochard* (to put it politely: 'Germanic spirit') that had, he thought, long been overvalued in French musical culture.[81] In other words, distasteful as it may be to find him invoking a 'vile seed' lodged within the French like 'tainted blood', for him such language denoted the same Wagnerian bombast later appropriated to National Socialist myths of Teutonic supremacy.[82] Even on this point, Debussy never rose to the extremes of those ideologues (including erstwhile *wagnéristes* like Maurice Barrès) for whom any performance of Wagner during the war amounted to treason.[83] Even after the deaths of several civilians from aerial bombardment had led him to flee Paris for Angers with his family he was able to opine with equanimity:

> As regards Wagner people are going to exaggerate! He retains the glory of having gathered together into a single recipe several centuries of music. That's surely something – and only a German was able to try it. Our mistake was to try for too long a time to follow his lead.[84]

In mid-October Debussy could even suggest casually that Wagner 'had enough genius that one might, little by little, forget his weaknesses as a man'.[85]

The thorny relation between aesthetics and politics aside, a stranger contradiction can be seen in the fact that Debussy, after asserting in late 1914 that 'never in any era have art and war been able to live comfortably together', was to enjoy, in late 1915, one last span of intense compositional creation.[86] The year had begun somewhat inauspiciously with the publication of the *Berceuse Héroïque*, Debussy's contribution to the collection of music and literature assembled by the *Daily Telegraph* in sympathy for Belgium's occupation by Germany. He seems to have seen this task as an unwelcome obligation. Echoing Baudelaire's line about 'military bands pouring heroism into the hearts of the citizens', he complained to Godet about the difficulty of using the Belgian national anthem, which 'pours no heroism into the hearts of those who were not brought up with it', and disparaged his *Berceuse* as 'all that I was able to do' in a state of physical weakness.[87]

Around the same time, he took editorial charge of a new complete edition of Chopin, one of several new publications of musical classics Durand launched to replace German editions. From his prefaces it is clear that Debussy found more than drudgery in this new role – indeed, the satisfaction in engaging closely with a compositional 'fellow spirit' emerges clearly from his description of Chopin as 'a delicious recounter of amorous or military legends, which often escape towards that forest of *As You Like It* where the fairies alone are mistresses of the imagination'.[88] At one point Dukas was led to wonder in a letter to a mutual friend whether 'the work as an editor has impaired that beautiful musical intuition that once guided him'.[89] But Dukas knew that other concerns were also contributing to Debussy's loss of 'assurance' at this time. His mother had long been seriously ill; on 23 March 1915 she died. Amidst his many expressions of pain at this loss, one of the most touching noted the impossibility of giving personal bereavement its due amidst widespread distress. 'The loss of my mother has affected me more heavily than I can say,' he confessed to Edgard Varèse, 'because I am well aware that in this moment there are tears for everyone.'[90]

During the weeks after the funeral, Debussy accompanied the eminent mezzo-soprano Claire Croiza in several of his songs at the first of many concerts for war charities with which he would be involved over the next few years. In May, he turned his editorial hand to the violin and harpsichord sonatas of Bach. But on the last day of June he wrote asking Durand how urgently he required the Bach edition, for he was sensing the germination of certain ideas whose cultivation promised relief from the 'long drought imposed on my brain by the war'.[91] Of the two works he mentioned, one, the ballet *Fêtes galantes*, was already familiar and would never be completed. The other was new. Eventually published as the triptych *En blanc et noir* for two pianos, it was to be the only substantial work in which Debussy took the risk, against his own strictures, of confronting the topic of war directly in his art.

The early working title of this triptych, *Caprices en blanc et noir*, acknowledged an inspiration in Francisco Goya's great series of etchings, the *Caprichos*. But Debussy later decided that this nod to a collection of images on the broad subject of human folly was not 'perfectly adapted to the genre of music it here designates, especially the second [piece], tragic and a little warlike'.[92] Indeed if neither the first nor the last piece of the triptych bears any particularly strong link to the historical context, the 'tragic and warlike' pose of the second attains a blatant topicality exceptional in the oeuvre. Dedicated to Durand's nephew Jacques Charlot, who had been killed in battle in March 1915, this central panel bears as an epigraph the *envoi* of François Villon's 'Ballad Against the Enemies of France'. The final two lines – 'Since those are not worthy to possess virtues / Who would wish ill of the kingdom of France' – link the piece to the desire Debussy expressed around the same time to prove that 'if there were 30 million *boches*, they would not destroy French thought, even after having tried to brutalize it before annihilating it.'[93]

The 'slow, sombre' opening pages of this piece – whose abrupt lurches of violent dissonance give rise to melancholy fanfares, then wisps of folk-like melody, then radiantly scored chordal revelations

– offer an apt pianistic translation of the universal accents of mourning traditionally heard in the 'last post' and funeral singing. But the later sections are more problematic. A turbulent 'battle scene' begins and soon becomes infected by what Debussy himself called the 'poisonous vapours' of the Lutheran choral 'Ein feste Burg'.[94] When this Germanic musical intruder eventually gives way before a radiant, *fortissimo* return of the initial fanfares, it is hard not to think that the occasion of war memorial has been deflected to bathetic narrative ends.

Years earlier, through similar spatial play with fanfares at the heart of his Dreyfus-era *Nocturnes*, Debussy had found a way to confront his listeners with unresolved questions about the affective lures of militant patriotism. Here, such interrogative and universalist aspirations seem to have been displaced in favour of faintly cartoonish topical propaganda. To be sure, this piece, like *Fêtes*, is but one 'panel' of a triptych; analysis of the whole could conceivably support a subtler interpretation.[95] But a few months later Debussy would give even more unambiguous expression to propagandistic sentiments in his final setting of words.

It would be misleading to list Debussy's last song, 'Noël pour les enfants qui n'ont pas une maison', in the artful lineage of poetic readings that had ended a couple of years earlier with the Mallarmé triptych. Nor indeed can the text he himself wrote for the 'Noël' – a pathetic hybrid of complaint and call to arms, sung by children who have lost all to the enemy – even claim as frail grounds of literary merit any of the cod-Symbolist inflections in the 1893 *Proses lyriques*. But perhaps that earlier, overwrought attempt by Debussy to be both poet and composer is the closest precursor in the song oeuvre to this last, frankly manipulative 'expression of sentiment', which shamelessly tugs the heartstrings on the reference to a 'poor dead mother' and whips up a frenzy for the last imprecation: 'give victory to the children of France!' There was surely some rueful cynicism in play when Debussy, informing

Dukas about the song's great success at various wartime charity concerts, again invoked Baudelaire to note how it 'entered into the hearts of the citizens'.[96]

If wartime patriotism can thus be said to have inspired, in the central panel of *En blanc et noir* and the 'Noël', a pair of extreme counter-examples to all those previous endorsements of suggestion over expression and esotericism over audience expectations, other productions of this same fertile year again add near-contradictory variety to the composite picture. A couple of days after signing the contract for *En blanc et noir* in early July, Debussy left Paris with his family for the seaside town of Pourville, near Dieppe. There, having 'recovered the possibility of thinking musically', he stayed for three months, composing 'like a madman, or like someone who is due to die the next day'.[97] Even as work continued on *En blanc et noir*, he completed twelve *Études* that set the capstone to his investigations of the piano's promises of private intoxication and public display. By early August he was also able to announce the completion of a sonata for cello and piano, the first of a projected group of six sonatas 'for various instruments'. Only a month later, work on a second sonata (eventually for flute, viola and harp) was also well advanced.

While each of these projects bears some faint verbal trace of Debussy's nationalistic inclinations, no individual etude or movement comes anywhere near the blatant contextual engagement of *En blanc et noir* or the 'Noël'. In the case of the etudes, the only nationalist gesture is a reverential reference in Debussy's whimsical preface to 'Our old Masters – I mean to say "our" admirable harpsichordists', meaning the great seventeenth- and eighteenth-century school of French harpsichord composers.[98] But this is but a passing nod in a paragraph whose primary intent is ostensibly to offer Debussy's excuse for not providing the performer of his *Études* any instructions about 'fingering'.

Perhaps this technical solicitude is in keeping with the musical aims of a volume that, absent overt indications of evocative intent, ostensibly unfolds as a series of dry technical studies ('for the five fingers'; 'for the repeated notes'; 'for the chords'). But it would be misleading to take this titular austerity as evidence of a move, on Debussy's part, towards the ideal of musical 'objectivity' that was to gain new prominence in all European arts during and after the First World War. In any careful hearing, it is possible to recognize in the *Études* a full gamut of familiar Debussyan 'characters' and poetic experiences – from music-hall wit through pastoral idyll; from distorted echoes of Romantic song and dance to 'escapes to the forest of *As You Like It*'. In other words, rather than signalling a disavowal of evocative intent, the blandly technical headings mark a further step beyond the elliptical 'after-titles' of the *Préludes* towards a reluctance to *specify* music's evocative implications. It is in this light that we can read the preface's closing exhortation, 'Let us search for our fingerings!', as an apt *envoi* to Debussy's whole mature pianistic oeuvre – that is, a final oblique invitation to the player to embark on an imaginative interrogation of the relationship between materials, techniques and sonorous poetry.

While none of the three chamber sonatas Debussy ultimately completed would bear a similar preface, all were published with a nationalistic signature on their title pages: '*Claude Debussy, Musicien Français*.' He clearly intended the signature to imply certain musical qualities, for he referred more than once to his attempt to recover an archetypically French 'suppleness' in form and 'grace' in expression from beneath the 'grandiloquence' of modern sonatas and 'epileptic' emotions of post-Wagnerian composition.[99] But while the concise proportions and delicacy of thought in all three sonatas loosely link them to seventeenth- or eighteenth-century models, to hear them in this light alone is to underplay the subtlety with which they combine 'antique' resonances with the post-Beethovenian principles Debussy had first elaborated in his *String Quartet* more than twenty years before.

Debussy obliquely acknowledged such historical perspective when he claimed that the longest, most colouristically distinctive second sonata reminded him 'of a very ancient Debussy – the one of the *Nocturnes*, it seems?'[100] This was an appropriate choice of reference. Effortlessly graceful as they might seem, the instrumental dialogues that unfurl across the three movements of the *Sonata for Flute, Viola and Harp* articulate Debussy's most intricately unified 'cyclic' structure since the orchestral triptych of 1897–9. Godet proved sensitive to this aspect when he described the sonata in classic organicist terms as a 'fruit . . . born complete from its cell, as life is made, from the inside to the outside'. But he also captured an essential difference between the sonata and the earlier triptych when, in describing the effect of its 'happy combination of timbres', his language became peppered with references to 'dreams', 'phantoms' and 'fantastic landscapes'; and to the 'echoes' and 'transpositions' that have 'volatilized' and 'confounded' all accents of reality within the magic of 'Debussyan "memory"'.[101]

Such florid language aptly registers the fact that this sonata, unlike the *Nocturnes*, enfolds no worldly materials as vivid and immediate in affect and association as a military march. The central section of the sonata's central movement releases instead one of Debussy's most breezily brilliant cascades of pastoral arabesques, supported by a delicate, euphonious harp murmur that deepens the sense of otherworldly idyll. Although a later, brief return to the same material reaches for more imploring tones, and the last movement soon begins on a stormier note, the radiantly affirmative close to the sonata stands as the clearest exemplar of the degree to which Debussy, even while reacting overtly to the war in the *Berceuse*, the 'Noël' and *En blanc et noir*, was able at the same time to effect a surprising degree of separation between life and art.

Debussy himself was to note this extreme separation with bemusement when finally announcing the hard-won completion of the third sonata (for violin and piano) in mid-1917, and observing to Godet that 'by an extremely human contradiction, it is full of joyous tumult.'[102] Beyond all the widely shared wartime anxieties, by that point he had yet more personal reasons for wonder at the 'joy' that spills infectiously from the three fleet, fine-boned movements of this sonata, his last significant composition. Those few months at Pourville in 1915 proved his last span of intense productivity. On his return to Paris, not only did he quickly lose the creative fluency he had recovered so briefly at the Normandy coast, but he soon received a first unambiguous, official diagnosis of the rectal cancer whose symptoms had been plaguing him for some time, and which was to kill him within less than three years.

It is clear that he was well aware of the seriousness of the diagnosis. Before his first surgery on 15 December 1915 he took the precaution of writing a farewell note to Emma: 'and you, my dear little one who will remain, love me in our little Chouchou . . . you are the only two souls who keep me from wishing to disappear without delay'.[103] An initial, somewhat flippant comparison of his own physical condition to that of an invaded *département* of France soon took on crueller poignancy when the initial phases of radium treatment in early 1916 left him feeling 'like a trench one defends for one hour, but which the sickness retakes the next hour'.[104] The new costs of treatment only further exacerbated longstanding financial difficulties; to make matters worse, even as he found Durand's generosity stretched to breaking point, his ex-wife Lilly secured a court judgement against him in July 1916 for his failure to pay her alimony for all of six years.

Surrounded by 'catastrophes', by late summer, when Emma and Chouchou had both also fallen ill with whooping-cough, Debussy

Debussy, visibly weakened by illness, with his daughter Chouchou at Moulleau in the Gironde, 1916.

felt that his own house was becoming more and more like the decrepit 'House of Usher' in the Poe opera he was still vainly struggling to complete. In mid-September, the family left Paris again to stay in a hotel near Arcachon on the Atlantic coast, whose atmosphere was considered beneficial for the lungs. Although Debussy was able to express some amusement at the 'stupefying *encores*' life was able to throw up (he had visited Arcachon in 1880 with Mme von Meck, and then again with Emma in late 1904 to escape the fuss about Lilly's suicide attempt), his sickness, coupled with irritations that included a young girl playing Franck incessantly on one of the hotel pianos, seems to have thwarted any renewed creative fluency.[105]

After the return to Paris, a plan to transform *Le Martyre de Saint-Sébastien* into an opera arose only to be postponed as excessively ambitious in his present state of health. The younger composer Darius Milhaud, who joined two colleagues to play the *Sonata for Flute, Viola and Harp* for Debussy *chez* Durand, left touching testimony to his frail condition at the time when recalling that in spite of his excitement at meeting a musician 'who occupied so important a place in his heart' he could not bring himself to mention his own music due to Debussy's 'ashen complexion and hands seized by a frail trembling'.[106] Even in this condition, however, Debussy was strong enough to continue participating in wartime charity concerts, including one on 21 December for the 'Clothing of the prisoners of war' – an organization with which Emma was closely involved – which featured, along with *En blanc et noir* and the inevitable 'Noël', two of his greatest song triptychs, *Chansons de Bilitis* and *Le promenoir des deux amants*, sung by Jane Bathori-Engel.

Early 1917 found Debussy, in his turn, begging for a bit of charity from Durand. An extreme cold snap was made all the more miserable by the fact that the occupation of the Northern *départements* had created a terrible shortage of coal in Paris. Debussy managed to secure brief respite in a way that showed some persistence of wit.

A merchant having undertaken to secure him some coal in return for an original composition, Debussy wrote for him what was to be both his last piece for piano and his last nod to the literary well-springs of so many accomplishments. Titling this slight, desperate offering with a line from Baudelaire's *Le Balcon*, 'The evenings illuminated by the glow of the coal', and seeding it with references to several piano preludes (including the Baudelairean 'Les sons et les parfums tournent dans l'air du soir'), Debussy made it both a whimsical nod to present woes and a compact node of 'Debussyan "memory"'.[107] But while it briefly had the desired effect – thanking the merchant, Debussy noted Chouchou's joy: 'in our time, little girls prefer sacks of coal to dolls!' – he was to be disappointed at the lack of further deliveries, and by the middle of March was again pleading for relief from the cold.[108]

In spite of such discomforts, during the same month Debussy managed to participate in further charity concerts even while continuing to wrestle with the 'terrible finale' of the violin sonata. As he suffered the ongoing freeze – and endured, as well, the rationing of sugar, milk and cheese; the constricted hours of the butchers; and the weekly two-day closures of the pastry shops – he found it in himself to quip to Durand that the inability to get hold of his favourite type of music paper 'is much more important than a couple of days without cakes'.[109] In May, while refusing an invitation from Fauré to perform his own *Études* due to a 'phobia' of having 'not enough fingers', he nonetheless felt able to accompany the violinist Gaston Poulet in the premiere of the violin sonata on a charity concert that also featured the Villon and Louÿs song triptychs, and the 'Noël', sung by Rose Féart. The sonata was not well received; a certain bitterness tinged Debussy's letter to the one musician who bothered to send a warm response: 'After all, musicians perhaps do not like music? or – more precisely, do they not like *my* music?'[110]

Perhaps this query gives plaintive evidence of an awareness that even in his spare and compact late sonatas – which bear some relationship to the 'neoclassical' tendencies soon to gain widespread prominence – Debussy was still, in some sense, out of step with the latest artistic trends. Although he attended the *Ballets russes* programme on 25 May, he left no record of his response to Diaghilev's latest *succès de scandale*, the ballet *Parade* with music by Satie and sets by Picasso. In fact, he had become estranged from Satie in recent years due in part to his resentment at the once-marginal composer's rise to prominence in younger avant-garde circles. In mid-1917, at any rate, he was still able to find some affirmation of his own continuing relevance in a brilliant performance of *La Mer* at the Société de la Conservatoire under the baton of Bernardino Molinari, a conductor he greatly admired.

A few days later, the family left for a last extended trip, to St-Jean-de-Luz in the French Basque country. Beyond its promises of warmth and peace, this locale was also chosen for its proximity to the house of Debussy's long-time collaborator Paul-Jean Toulet, with whom he had recently revived exchanges on their proposed adaptation of *As You Like It*. But the project did not go as smoothly as hoped. As Emma reported, in the lassitude of his illness Debussy found the 'nervousness' of his collaborator wearying.[111] (Emma attributed Toulet with a 'mysterious malady'; Debussy described him more simply as an alcoholic.) With his usual acerbic perspective on travel, Debussy wrote to Godet of the 'little mountains without pretension', and the nearby bay 'where some people who could conceivably be less ugly go to bathe, and where a coal-boat rests, useful but ruining the horizon'. A more telling indication of his mood was the little poem he quoted before signing off. One of his favourite poets, Jules Laforgue, had provided him a gloomy, oft-repeated late refrain: 'I am toiling in the factories of nothingness.' Now Laforgue also became the source of four slightly misquoted lines, grim testimony to the latest depths of fatalism: 'The dead / It is discreet / They sleep / Well in the cold.'[112]

Further performances of the violin sonata at charity concerts in St-Jean-de-Luz and Biarritz fared little better than the Parisian premiere – indeed one critic now trumped Debussy's comparisons of his sick body to a war-scarred landscape when claiming to hear in the sonata 'the impression of the Somme or something else similarly devastated'.[113] If it is hard to understand how a work in which Godet heard a 'simple and direct accent that denotes the good will to banter with brothers of all ages' could inspire such dark imagery, it is possible the critic was responding more to the precariousness of the performance than to the composition itself.[114] As Emma recalled on returning to Paris in October, she had been desperately worried about whether or not her exhausted husband would make it to the end of the concert.

For his part, Debussy may have found his return from a trip whose 'three long months' had passed, this time, leaving 'nothing behind them' somewhat lightened by the letters Godet sent, full of fulsome praise, after his latest voyages through Debussy's music.[115] As he toiled on *La Boîte à joujoux* (a work, he affirmed, 'conceived in a wholly French spirit') and the opera version of *Le Martyre*, he would surely have been touched to find enclosed in one of these missives a copy of a letter Godet had received from a frontline soldier for whom Debussy's music remained one of the finest products of the *patrie* he was defending with his life.[116] But however such an affirmation may have satisfied Debussy's own nationalist leanings, it could hardly have provided much lasting consolation in the rapidly worsening health that largely confined him to his bed through another cold winter, of 1917–18.

In a few last, near-indecipherable letters to Emma, Debussy, in spite of his 'sadly constrained' condition, did his best to honour the tradition of bidding her New Year's greeting. Through January and February, as he managed at Godet's behest to undertake detailed revisions to the *Nocturnes* for a performance in Switzerland conducted by Ernest Ansermet, her letters recorded his constantly worsening condition and her desperation at the little she could do to help. Even in these terminal phases of illness, there were still thoughts of official honours. In mid-March, husband and wife both sought, through the 'perpetual secretary' of the Académie des Beaux-Arts, Charles-Marie Widor, to secure Debussy's election to the chair Widor himself had vacated at the Académie years before. But the way remained barred due to the intransigence of Camille Saint-Saëns, who had received *En blanc et noir* as the latest of the composer's 'atrocities' – worthy, he put it, of standing 'alongside cubist paintings'.[117]

As Laloy reported it, on his last visit on 21 March Debussy was able to express breezy regret – 'say hello to Monsieur Castor!' – at his inability to attend the staging of Rameau's opera *Castor et Pollux*, which was proceeding in spite of German bombardments.[118] A few days later, a last visit from Durand found Debussy in distress at the danger he was causing others due to his inability to descend with them to the basement – and fully aware, as he requested a last cigarette, that 'it was only a question of hours'.[119] Somehow the next day, on 24 March, he found the energy to write to the president of the Institut de France in support of his candidacy to the Académie. By the next evening he was dead. Of the fifty or so people who gathered at the house for the funeral procession many were to peel away into streets still tense from continuing bombardments, leaving barely twenty to observe the temporary interment in the Père-Lachaise cemetery. Later, Debussy's remains were moved back closer to home, to lie in the Passy Cemetery not far from the Bois.

Epilogue

Within months of Debussy's death at least one leading polemicist was already eager to begin relegating him to outmoded history. In late 1918 the polymath artist and writer Jean Cocteau, who had brought Picasso and Satie together for the ballet *Parade*, urged in his pamphlet *Le Coq et l'arlequin* for a restoration of pure French values (the Cock) after excessive reliance on foreign influences (the Harlequin). For Cocteau, even the late *musicien français* had fallen afoul of 'harlequin' tendencies:

> Debussy went astray, because from the German pit he fell into the Russian trap. Once again, the pedal melts the rhythm, creates a sort of fluid ambience friendly to *myopic ears*. Satie remains intact. Listen to his *Gymnopédies*, so clean in their line and their melancholy. Debussy orchestrates them, befogs them, envelops the exquisite architecture in a cloud. . . . Satie speaks of Ingres; Debussy transposes Claude Monet *à la Russe*.[1]

The glib simplification of Debussy's negotiations amidst various influences aside, there is something snidely opportunistic about Cocteau's use of those slight orchestral arrangements as primary support for his invidious distinction between Satie's Ingresque neo-classicism and Debussy's music in the style of Monet. The association that had first arisen in the Institut's reactionary critique of 'vague, Impressionist' tendencies recurs here as one more counter in a game of avant-garde rhetoric.

While the ideals hailed in *The Cock* were to be abundantly exemplified by some of Satie's musical followers, not everyone in the immediate post-war years saw a similar need to disavow Debussy. One countervailing view emerged a couple of years later when the young musicologist Henry Prunières devoted the second, December 1920 issue of his new journal *La Revue Musicale* to a special issue in the composer's memory.[2] Prunières chose to begin the issue with a panegyric by his friend André Suarès whose nationalistic inflections seem like a direct rebuttal to Cocteau:

> If French music is at present, just as it was in the lively Middle Ages and the tumultuous times of the early Renaissance, the example and the model for all Europe, we truly owe this only to Debussy alone. He has renewed everything: the sung poem; piano music; and the musical drama.[3]

Not all the contributors (some of whom were foreign) were content to echo Suarès's nationalistic inflections. But most, adopting similarly hagiographic tones about Debussy's generic 'renewals', also felt a need to reject Cocteau's casual 'Impressionist' indictment and insist instead on the literary qualities of Debussy's imagination.

If Suarès's blithe assertion that Debussy was 'the Rimbaud of music' now seems a mere curiosity, Godet's emphasis in his contribution on the 'six great French voices' central to his song writing – Verlaine, Baudelaire and Mallarmé; Villon, d'Orléans, and l'Hermite – clearly rests on stronger ground.[4] But Godet's primary aim was simply to insist that, in contrast to any 'realistic' intent, 'the *Debussyste* kind of naturalism . . . is essentially "expressive".'[5] Suarès had put the same point more crudely when claiming that 'Debussy sees nothing all around him but emotion.'[6] Alfred Cortot, picking up the thread in an essay on the piano music, adds nuance:

> It is rare to find at the basis of his inspiration one of those sentiments that, since the Beethovenian revelation, has moved the soul of composers as it animates their works, that is to say the human passions, woes or enthusiasms. This is not to say that he repudiates or disdains musical emotion, but, by means of a sort of aristocratic reserve, he would rather suggest it to us obliquely than make us feel it directly.[7]

In this light, Cortot suggests, Debussy's music 'demands a more literary and more nuanced imaginative collaboration than any previous music'.[8]

All this defensive hyperbole about Debussyan 'emotion' might now seem trivial and *passé*. But it can be taken as symptomatic of central emerging concerns of the post-Debussyan musical era. A telling illustration of the issues at stake can be found by leafing through the last pages of the memorial issue to the musical supplement appended under the title *Tombeau de Claude Debussy*. This musical 'tomb' gathers, behind a lithographic title page by Raoul Dufy, ten works dedicated to Debussy by notable contemporaries. As if to exemplify Suarès's sense of pan-European impact, it includes, alongside music by Frenchmen Dukas, Ravel and Satie, eminent representatives of Hungary (Bartók), Spain (de Falla), Russia (Stravinsky), Italy (Malipiero) and Britain (Goossens).

Given that only some wrote expressly for the *Tombeau* and others contributed work in progress, the collection projects a somewhat haphazard air. For one thing, it gives strangely little room to compositional 'reading'. After opening with a piano piece by Dukas, '*La plainte, au loin, du faune . . .*', which refers pointedly to Debussy's Mallarmé *Prélude*, it closes with its only song – ironically, written 'In Memory of an admiring and warm friendship of thirty years' by Cocteau's hero Satie. The imagery in the Lamartine poem Satie set in this little song might be said to let the cliché about 'nature painting' in by the back door:

> What use to me these valleys, these palaces, these cottages,
> Vain objects from which for me the charm has flown?
> Rivers, rocks, forests, solitudes so precious,
> One single soul is missing and everything is depopulated!

Hints of proto-Impressionist scenery aside, however, the song is startling for its intense personal appeal. Expressive *crescendi* through the second and fourth lines reach something like a visceral cry for the last word, giving powerful voice to the emotion Godet and others had heard as central to Debussy's musical art.

Such quasi-ritualistic anguish was of course perfectly appropriate to a *Tombeau*. But to leaf through the collection again with an eye for expressive force rather than literary attunement is to find that a different piece now stands out from all the others. Dukas, Roussel and Goossens pepper their contributions with *espressivo* ('expressive') indications and dynamic markings; De Falla and Bartók summon a *mesto* ('mournful') mood; even Ravel's *Duo for violin and cello*, later to become a sonata movement in the spirit of Debussy's last chamber works, does not take its classicizing pose so far as to efface all invitations to expressive sensitivity. The seventh contribution is the exception. Stravinsky's *Fragment from the Symphonies of Wind Instruments . . . in memory of C. A. Debussy* bears no dynamic indications and few phrase marks on its two pages of austere piano chords. Absent any invitation to mourn, or any hints to help a 'literary and imaginative collaboration', it gives only a metronome marking as guidance to the performer.

This work was actually an appropriate offering to Debussy's tomb, for it was modelled on the music for the Russian Orthodox office of the dead. But while Stravinsky referred to the *Symphonies*, early on, in aptly expressive terms – 'austere ritual'; 'short litanies'; soft 'chanting' – these traditional, humane roots were subsequently lost from view as the piece gained iconic status, aided by Stravinsky's later polemics for an anti-expressive aesthetic, as a precursor of high-modernist musical abstraction.[9] In the view of Stravinsky expert Richard Taruskin, the highly influential, deliberately revisionist reception history of this and many other major products of the 'Russian period' can be seen to exemplify the gradual hardening of a quintessentially modernist approach to *all* music as 'the music itself' – that is, as pure sound patterns, just as bleached of emotive or social powers as those two stark pages in the *Tombeau de Claude Debussy*.[10]

Taruskin too has his polemical investments. But even so, the historiographical resonance he sees in those two pages can invite reflection, for example, about the fact that Boulez could affirm that 'modern music awakens in the afternoon of a faun' in a few paragraphs whose paeans to the formal freedom and orchestral imagination of the *Prélude* include minimal reference to poetry or agonistic post-*wagnérisme*; or about how Barraqué's discussion of the thought-like fluidity of the 'theme-objects' and 'structural relations' in *La Mer* could so underplay the visceral force and affective depth of the work's tidal surges, whirling waltzes and post-Romantic inflections.[11] If anything, such questions come even more insistently to mind in the face of the extreme schematic abstraction of some prominent late-twentieth-century analytical approaches to Debussy's music – which occasionally bring to mind his report to Laloy of a discussion with their mutual friend Jean Marnold: 'Music, it is all numbers, he said to me. And you are another, I was tempted to respond.'[12]

Still, the fact that Marnold himself could follow his assertively formalist response to the *Nocturnes* with an extravagantly anthropomorphic account of *La Mer* can be taken as a reminder that the full range of Debussyan criticism has always been even more heterogeneous than the music in the 1920 *Tombeau*. Latterly, it seems that simplistic 'representational' assumptions and aridly scientistic approaches alike are finally being balanced by critical reflections of a more nuanced, cultural-historical and literary-critical sensitivity.

Debussy's work table with the manuscript of *Pelléas et Mélisande*.

Arguably, this kind of approach has the potential to restore to a hearing of this exquisitely literary musical art some of the Baudelairean and Mallarméan depths so often effaced by modernist technocratic methods.

Any considered exploration of these latest developments being impractical here, it might nonetheless be possible to adumbrate their promise, in conclusion, by glancing back before Boulez and Barraqué and Prunières and Cocteau into a stage of reception Debussy himself would have been able to appreciate. No doubt the consolatory letters Godet wrote him during the war carry some of the same hagiographic hyperbole later inscribed into the memorial issue of *La Revue musicale*. But when he extravagantly compared Debussy's music, at one point, to a 'bath that cures, by enchantment, all wounds', he did so in words that can serve as a lasting summons to seek in his music some kind of mediation of the very terms that have remained central to debates about his historical significance:

> Whenever my mind, always running a bit behind my sensibility, despairs of accompanying it through its modulations and I find myself like a man forced to jump over difficult hurdles, you intervene . . . a stroke of the baton . . . and *voilà*: harmony is established between head and heart (and indeed, at the same time, between the two worlds that compose our universe of men: that which we see outside of us, and think about; that which, from within, reacts, and which one feels).[13]

Whether or not Godet exaggerates the magical powers of Debussy's baton, his image of a frail bridge between 'two worlds' succinctly encapsulates the questions that can still be heard within the sounds it once inspired.

References

Introduction

1 Claude Debussy, *Correspondance: 1872–1918*, ed. François Lesure and Denis Herlin (Paris, 2005), p. 1313. All translations are my own unless otherwise indicated.
2 Claude Debussy, *Monsieur Croche et Autres Écrits*, ed. François Lesure, 2nd edn (Paris, 1987), pp. 52–3.
3 E. Vuillermoz, 'Le monument de Claude Debussy à Paris', unpaginated article in the programme for a dedicatory concert at the Théâtre de Champs-Elysées, 17 June 1932. My thanks to Alexandra Laederich, Curator of the Centre de Documentation Claude Debussy in Paris.
4 Debussy, *Correspondance*, p. 586.

1 A Music that Clothes the Poetry

1 François Lesure, *Claude Debussy: Biographie Critique* (Paris, 1994), p. 15.
2 Ibid., p. 18.
3 Ibid., p. 21.
4 A fifth child, born in 1873, died in 1877.
5 See e.g. the reminiscences of Camille Bellaigue and Gabriel Pierné quoted in Léon Vallas, *Claude Debussy: His Life and Works*, trans. Maire and Grace O'Brien (Oxford, 1933), p. 6.
6 Lesure, *Claude Debussy*, p. 25.
7 Maurice Emmanuel, *Pelléas et Mélisande de Claude Debussy*, 2nd edn (Paris, 1950), p. 11.
8 Ibid., p. 12.

9 Lesure, *Claude Debussy*, p. 29.
10 Emmanuel, *Pelléas et Mélisande*, p. 17.
11 Claude Debussy, *Monsieur Croche et Autres Écrits*, 2nd edn, ed. François Lesure (Paris, 1987), p. 65.
12 Vallas, *Claude Debussy*, p. 9.
13 Edward Lockspeiser, *Debussy: His Life and Mind* (London, 1962), vol. I, p. 207.
14 Lesure, *Claude Debussy*, p. 39.
15 Gabriel Pierné and Paul Vidal, 'Souvenirs d'Achille Debussy', *Revue musicale*, VII (1 May 1926), pp. 10–16, at 12.
16 Only one page of music for 'Madrid' survives, without words; the other song is lost.
17 Lesure, *Claude Debussy*, p. 43.
18 Emmanuel, *Pelléas et Mélisande*, p. 19.
19 Edward Lockspeiser, 'Debussy, Tchaikovsky and Madame von Meck', *The Musical Quarterly*, XXII (1936), pp. 38–44, at p. 39.
20 Ibid., p. 41.
21 No copy of the *Swan Lake* arrangements published in Russia has been discovered. See Lockspeiser, *Debussy*, pp. 46–7.
22 Ibid., p. 46.
23 On this point, see André Schaeffner, 'Debussy et ses Rapports avec la Musique Russe', in his *Essais de musicologie* (Paris, 1980).
24 This, at any rate, is how she identified him to Tchaikovsky. See Lockspeiser, 'Debussy, Tchaikovsky, and Madame von Meck', p. 38.
25 Vallas, *Claude Debussy*, p. 20; Emmanuel, *Pelléas et Mélisande*, pp. 20–21.
26 Lesure, *Claude Debussy*, p. 48.
27 Ibid., p. 37.
28 See Lockspeiser, *Debussy*, pp. 66–7.
29 This is the dedication for the unpublished song 'Tragédie' on words by Léon Valade. See Margaret G. Cobb, ed., Richard Miller, trans., *The Poetic Debussy: A Collection of His Song Texts and Selected Letters*, 2nd edn (Rochester, 1994), p. 29.
30 Lesure, *Claude Debussy*, p. 53
31 Edward Lockspeiser, 'Claude Debussy Dans la Correspondance de Tchaikovsky et de Mme von Meck', *Revue musicale*, XVIII (November 1937), pp. 217–21, at p. 218.

32 Georges Favre, *Compositeurs français méconnues* (Paris, 1983), pp. 36–7.
33 Lesure, *Claude Debussy*, p. 60.
34 Ibid., p. 61.
35 Pierné and Vidal, 'Souvenirs d'Achille Debussy', p. 15.
36 See e.g. the recollections quoted in Lesure, *Claude Debussy*, pp. 66–8.
37 Claude Debussy, *Correspondance: 1872–1918*, ed. F. Lesure and D. Herlin (Paris, 2005), p. 1015.
38 Lesure, *Claude Debussy*, p. 69.
39 Debussy, *Monsieur Croche*, p. 189.
40 Debussy, *Correspondance*, p. 29.
41 See for example Mallarmé's letter to his friend Cazalis of 28 April 1866, in Stéphane Mallarmé, *Oeuvres complètes*, ed. Bertrand Marchal (Paris, 1998), p. 696.
42 Debussy, *Correspondance*, p. 43.
43 Ibid., p. 29.
44 Ibid., p. 49.
45 Ibid., p. 46.
46 Ibid., p. 25; p. 27.
47 Ibid., p. 33.
48 Ibid., p. 45.
49 Lesure, *Claude Debussy*, p. 84.
50 Debussy, *Correspondance*, p. 1927.
51 Pierné and Vidal, 'Souvenirs d'Achille Debussy', p. 15.
52 Debussy, *Correspondance*, pp. 51–4.
53 Ibid., p. 59.
54 Trans. in Vallas, *Debussy*, p. 42.
55 Debussy, *Correspondance*, p. 59.
56 Ibid., pp. 61–2.
57 Ibid., p. 64, n. 4.
58 See Richard Langham Smith, 'Debussy and the Pre-Raphaelites', *19th-century Music*, v/2 (1981), pp. 95–109.
59 Claude Debussy, *Correspondance*, p. 70, n. 5.
60 See for example the famous book by Seurat's student Paul Signac, *D'Eugène Delacroix au néo-Impressionisme* (Paris, 1899).
61 For a reproduction of Debussy's completed questionnaire, see Roger Nichols, *The Life of Debussy* (Cambridge, 1998), p. 70.

62 A key reference point is Baudelaire's oft-reprinted 1861 essay 'Richard Wagner et *Tannhäuser* à Paris'. On this much-discussed aspect of the songs see for example Robin Holloway, *Debussy and Wagner* (London, 1979), pp. 42–9.
63 Louise Liebich, *Claude-Achille Debussy* (London, 1908), p. 33.
64 Debussy playfully acknowledged the change in a letter to Robert Godet, *Correspondance*, p. 77.
65 Holloway, *Debussy and Wagner*, p. 42.
66 Debussy, *Monsieur Croche*, p. 229; Robert Godet, 'En marge de la marge', *La Revue musicale*, VII (1926), pp. 51–86, at p. 55.
67 Debussy, *Correspondance*, p. 78.
68 Lockspeiser, *Debussy*, p. 205.
69 Ibid., p. 206.
70 Ibid., p. 207.
71 See for example Richard Mueller, 'Javanese Influence on Debussy's *Fantaisie* and Beyond', *19th-century Music*, x/2 (1986), pp. 157–86.
72 Debussy, *Correspondance*, p. 87.
73 Ibid., p. 1204.
74 Mendès also provided financial support for the engraving of the *Fantaisie*.
75 Lockspeiser, *Debussy*, p. 205.
76 Paul Dukas, *Correspondance*, ed. Georges Favre (Paris, 1971), p. 21.
77 Vallas, *Claude Debussy*, p. 77.
78 Debussy, *Correspondance*, p. 103.
79 René Peter, *Claude Debussy*, 2nd edn (Paris, 1944), p. 32.
80 Lesure, *Claude Debussy*, p. 115.

2 A Dream from Which One Draws Back the Veils

1 This and the next several quotes are drawn from Claude Debussy, *Correspondance: 1872–1918*, ed. François Lesure and Denis Herlin (Paris, 2005), pp. 113–17.
2 Only the first two were published, in October 1892, in the *Entretiens politiques et littéraires*.
3 On Seurat's representation of a new culture of leisure see for example T. J. Clark, *The Painting of Modern Life: Paris in the Art of Manet and*

His Followers (Princeton, NJ, 1984), pp. 261–8.

4 Debussy, *Correspondance*, p. 112.

5 Ibid., p. 120, n. 2.

6 Ibid., p. 126.

7 Ibid., p. 129.

8 Ibid., p. 131.

9 Ibid., p. 1098.

10 Paul Dukas, *Correspondance*, ed. Georges Favre (Paris, 1971), p. 21.

11 Debussy, *Correspondance*, p. 157.

12 Ibid., p. 160.

13 Ibid., p. 155.

14 Ibid., p. 161.

15 Ibid., p. 157.

16 See Gordon Millan, *Pierre Louÿs ou le culte de l'amitié* (Aix-en-Provence, 1979), p. 212; and Pierre Louÿs, *Milles lettres inédites de Pierre Louÿs à Georges Louis 1890–1917* (Paris, 2002), p. 1016.

17 Debussy, *Correspondance*, p. 176.

18 See François Lesure, *Claude Debussy: Biographie Critique* (Paris, 1994), p. 144.

19 Debussy, *Correspondance*, p. 192

20 Ibid., pp. 174–5.

21 Ibid., p. 191.

22 Ibid., pp. 196–8.

23 See Vincent d'Indy, *Cours de Composition Musicale* (Paris, 1903–50).

24 See David J. Code, 'Debussy's String Quartet in the Brussels Salon of *La Libre Esthétique*', *19th-Century Music*, XXX/3 (Spring 2007), pp. 257–87.

25 The review appeared in the *Guide Musical* of 4 March. See Léon Vallas, *Claude Debussy: His Life and Works*, trans. Maire and Grace O'Brien (Oxford, 1933), p. 98.

26 See Madeleine Octave Maus, *Trente années de lutte pour l'art: Les XX et La Libre Esthétique 1884–1914* (Brussels, 1926).

27 Debussy, *Correspondance*, p. 200.

28 Quoted in Pasteur Vallery-Radot, *Tel était Claude Debussy* (Paris, 1958), pp. 41–3.

29 Debussy, *Correspondance*, p. 217.

30 Ibid., p. 351.

31 René Peter, *Claude Debussy*, 2nd edn (Paris, 1944), p. 53.

32 Debussy, *Correspondance*, pp. 218–19; p. 215.

33 Ibid., p. 222.

34 Claude Debussy, *Monsieur Croche et Autres Écrits*, ed. François Lesure, 2nd edn (Paris, 1987), p. 293.

35 Marcel Dietschy, *A Portrait of Claude Debussy*, ed. and trans. William Ashbrook and Margaret G. Cobb (Oxford, 1990), p. 93.

36 Lesure, *Claude Debussy*, p. 158.

37 Debussy, *Correspondance*, p. 278.

38 Ibid., p. 229.

39 Ibid., p. 229.

40 Ibid., p. 286.

41 Pierre Boulez, *Relevés d'Apprenti* (Paris, 1966), p. 336.

42 Peter, *Claude Debussy*, p. 76.

43 See David J. Code, 'The Formal Rhythms of Mallarmé's Faun', *Representations* LXXXVI (Spring 2004), pp. 76–119.

44 See David J. Code, 'Hearing Debussy Reading Mallarmé: Music *après Wagner* in the *Prélude à l'après-midi d'un faune*', *Journal of the American Musicological Society*, LIV/3 (2001), pp. 493–554.

45 Hector Berlioz, *Grand traité d'instrumentation et d'orchestration modernes* (Paris, 1843)

46 See for example Alfred Lavignac, *Le Voyage Artistique à Bayreuth* (Paris, 1897).

47 Carolyn Abbate, '*Tristan* in the Composition of *Pelléas*', *19th-century Music*, V/2 (1981), pp. 117–41, at p. 138.

48 Universal Classics released a CD under this title in 1995, subtitled 'Music to Caress Your Innermost Thoughts'.

49 On the formal 'suspension' typical of Virgilian pastoral, see for example Paul Alpers, *What is Pastoral?* (Chicago, IL, 1996).

50 Debussy, *Correspondance*, p. 270.

51 See Denis Herlin, 'Une oeuvre inachevée: *La Saulaie*', *Cahiers Debussy*, XX (1996), pp. 3–23.

52 H. P. Clive, *P. Louÿs (1870–1925): A Biography* (Oxford, 1978), p. 551.

53 Debussy, *Correspondance*, p. 551.

54 Ibid., p. 330.

55 The collection was reprinted several times by the end of the century, both in the original and in several translations.

56 Oscar Thompson, *Debussy: Man and Artist*, 2nd edn (New York, 1967), p. 110.
57 Debussy, *Correspondance*, pp. 425–6.
58 See Schiller, 'Über naïve und sentimentalische Dichtung', in *Friedrich Schiller: Werke und Briefe*, ed. Otto Dann et al., vol. VIII (Frankfurt am Main, 1992), pp. 706–810.
59 The scale known as the 'whole-tone scale' (because it consists of six whole steps) became specifically associated with Debussy due to the exceptional frequency with which he used it, although he was far from the only composer to do so.
60 Debussy, *Correspondance*, p. 326.
61 Debussy, *Monsieur Croche*, p. 52.
62 Debussy, *Correspondance*, p. 62.
63 Debussy, *Monsieur Croche*, p. 63.
64 See Debussy, *Correspondance*, p. 313 n. 1; p. 343 n. 6. The collaboration with René Peter resulted in a complete draft of one play, *Frèresen Art*, which was never performed, and only discovered after Debussy's death. For a brief discussion see Jane Fulcher, *French Cultural Politics and Music: From the Dreyfus Affair to the First World War* (Oxford, 1999), pp. 174–5.
65 Lesure, *Claude Debussy*, p. 185.
66 See an example in Lockspeiser, *Debussy*, p. 131.
67 Debussy, *Correspondance*, p. 394.
68 For a critical polemic along these lines from Satie's later champion see Jean Cocteau, *Le Coq et l'arlequin: Notes autour de la musique* (Paris, 1918).
69 Lesure, *Claude Debussy*, p. 185.
70 Debussy, *Correspondance*, p. 343.
71 Ibid., p. 418.
72 Ibid., p. 380; p. 394; p. 398.
73 Ibid., p. 400.
74 Ibid., p. 419.
75 Jean Marnold, 'Les "Nocturnes" de Claude Debussy', *Le Courrier musical*, v/5 (1 March 1902), pp. 68–71.
76 Thompson, *Debussy*, pp. 319–20.
77 'The Chinese scale' was a common term for what is now termed the pentatonic. See for example Mallarmé's early poem 'Las de l'amer

repos', whose lyric persona wishes to 'forsake the ravenous Art of cruel lands' and emulate the 'Chinese of fine and limpid soul'.

78 See Claude Debussy, *Nocturnes*, ed. Denis Herlin. *Oeuvres complètes*, série v, vol. 3 (Paris, 1999), p. xxvii.

79 See 'Les Petites Vielles' ('The Little Old Women') in *Les Fleurs du mal*.

80 Debussy, *Monsieur Croche*, p. 46.

81 Debussy, *Correspondance*, p. 585.

82 Debussy, *Nocturnes*, ed. Herlin, p. xxii.

83 See Rosamonde Sanson, *Les 14 Juillet (1789–1935)* (Paris, 1976).

84 See James R. Lehning, *To Be A Citizen: The Political Culture of the Early French Third Republic* (Ithaca, NY, 2001).

85 For the 'carnivalesque' as a trope transmitted into nineteenth-century art through Goethe, see Mikhail Bakhtin, *Rabelais and his World*, trans. Hélène Iswolsky (Bloomington, IN, 1984), pp. 244–56.

86 See Debussy, *Correspondance*, p. 395; Urbain Gohier, *L'Armée contre la Nation* (Paris, 1898); Ferdinand Brunétière, *La Nation et L'Armée* (Paris, 1899).

87 Debussy, *Correspondance*, p. 347.

88 Ibid., p. 446.

89 Ibid., p. 468; p. 477.

90 Ibid., p. 531.

91 Lesure, *Claude Debussy*, p. 194.

92 Debussy, *Correspondance*, p. 538.

93 Ibid., p. 539.

94 Ibid., p. 549, n. 1.

95 Paul Dukas, *Écrits sur la musique*, ed. Gustave Samazeuilh (Paris, 1948), p. 502.

96 Debussy, *Correspondance*, p. 553.

97 Ibid., p. 559.

3 The Art of a Curious Savage

1 Claude Debussy, *Monsieur Croche et Autres Écrits*, ed. François Lesure, 2nd edn (Paris, 1987), p. 23.

2 Ibid., p. 60; p. 97.

3 Ibid., p. 150.

4 Ibid., p. 29.

5 Claude Debussy, *Correspondance: 1872–1918*, ed. F. Lesure and D. Herlin (Paris, 2005), p. 596.

6 Albert Carré, *Souvenirs de théâtre*, ed. Robert Favart (Paris, 1950), p. 277.

7 *Le Figaro*, 13 April 1902.

8 Cited in René Peter, *Claude Debussy* (Paris, 1944), pp. 176–7.

9 Romain Rolland, *Richard Strauss et Romain Rolland: Correspondance, Fragments de Journal* (Paris, 1951), p. 160.

10 Ibid., p. 159.

11 Maurice Emmanuel, *Pelléas et Mélisande de Claude Debussy*, 2nd edn (Paris, 1950), p. 78.

12 Joseph Kerman, *Opera as Drama* (New York, 1952), p. 175.

13 Emmanuel, *Pelléas et Mélisande*, p. 89.

14 Adolphe Jullien, 'Théâtre national de l'Opéra-comique: *Pelléas et Mélisande*', *Le Théâtre*, LXXXIV (June 1902), pp. 5–15, at p. 5.

15 See Roger Nichols and Richard Langham Smith, *Claude Debussy: Pelléas et Mélisande* (Cambridge, 1989), p. 65.

16 Debussy, *Correspondance*, p. 220.

17 Maurice Maeterlinck, 'Sur les Femmes', in his *Le Trésor des Humbles*, 42nd edn (Paris, 1904), pp. 81–98, at p. 96.

18 For more on the work's allegorical implications, see Katherine Bergeron, 'Mélisande's Hair, or, The Trouble in Allemonde: A Postmodern Allegory at the Opéra-comique', in *Siren Songs: Representations of Gender and Sexuality in Opera*, ed. Mary Ann Smart (Princeton, NJ, 2000), pp. 160–85.

19 Carolyn Abbate, '*Tristan* in the Composition of *Pelléas*', *19th-century Music*, v/2 (1981), pp. 117–41.

20 Debussy, *Correspondance*, p. 642.

21 André Messager, 'Les premières représentations de *Pelléas*', *La Revue musicale*, VII/7 (1 May 1926), pp. 112–13.

22 Debussy, *Monsieur Croche*, p. 276.

23 Paul Dukas, *Écrits sur la musique*, ed. Gustave Samazeuilh (Paris, 1948), p. 575.

24 *Le Temps*, 20 May 1902.

25 Pierre Boulez, *Orientations*, ed. Jean-Jacques Nattiez, trans. Martin Cooper (London, 1986), p. 306; Emmanuel, *Pelléas et Mélisande*, p. 213.

26 Debussy, *Correspondance*, p. 679.
27 Ibid., p. 668.
28 Ibid., p. 736.
29 Ibid., p. 758.
30 Ibid., p. 779.
31 See the gently corrective letter of February 1906 to Pierre Lalo in Maurice Ravel, *Lettres, Écrits, Entretiens*, ed. Arbie Orenstein (Paris, 1989), p. 83.
32 Guido Gatti, 'The Piano Works of Claude Debussy', *Musical Quarterly*, VII/3 (1921), pp. 418–60, at p. 422.
33 Debussy, *Correspondance*, p. 1212. The comment partly reflected the experience of living close to the railway that once encircled Paris.
34 Ibid., p. 1119.
35 Ibid., p. 1211.
36 The anomalous inclusion of more than one poet in a song triptych was to be partly mitigated a few years later when Debussy republished the l'Hermite song, 'La Grotte', as one of a triptych on texts by the same poet.
37 Debussy, *Correspondance*, p. 859.
38 The *Trois Chansons de France* were also dedicated to her – but more discreetly, as 'Mme S. Bardac'.
39 Debussy, *Correspondance*, p. 848.
40 Ibid., p. 854; p. 858; p. 861.
41 Ibid., p. 865; p. 872.
42 Ibid., p. 901.
43 See Gordon Millan, *Pierre Louÿs ou le culte de l'amitié* (Aix-en-Provence, 1979), p. 252.
44 Debussy, *Correspondance*, p. 896; p. 917.
45 Jean Lorrain, *Pelléastres* (Paris, 1910).
46 See Marcel Dietschy, *A Portrait of Claude Debussy*, ed. and trans. William Ashbrook and Margaret G. Cobb (Oxford, 1990), pp. 133–4.
47 See again the conversation with Guiraud, in Edward Lockspeiser, *Debussy: His Life and Mind* (London, 1962), vol. I, p. 208.
48 Debussy, *Monsieur Croche*, p. 49.
49 Jean Barraqué, *Debussy*, 2nd edn, ed. François Lesure (Paris, 1994), pp. 182–4.

50 Louis Schneider, 'Les Concerts Classiques', *Gil blas*, 15 October 1905, p. 3.
51 Louis Laloy, 'Concerts Chevillard: *La Mer*, trois esquisses symphoniques de Claude Debussy [...]', *Mercure musical*, 1 November 1905, p. 487.
52 Jean Marnold, 'Concerts Lamoureux – Claude Debussy: *La Mer*', *Le Mercure de France*, LVIII (1905) pp. 131–5, at 134.
53 Bruneau, *Le Figaro*, 16 October 1905; Carraud, 'Les Concerts', *La Liberté*, 17 October 1905, p. 3.
54 *Le Temps*, 14 October 1905.
55 Debussy, *Correspondance*, p. 928.
56 Ibid., p. 929.
57 Ibid., p. 919.
58 Ibid., p. 778.
59 Ibid., p. 1002; p. 1027.
60 Ibid., p. 1027.
61 Ibid., p. 668.
62 Ibid., p. 1020.
63 See the scornful remarks by 'l'Ouvreuse' in *Comoedia*, 4 November 1907.
64 Debussy, *Correspondance*, 1055.
65 *Comoedia*, 20 January 1908.
66 Debussy, *Correspondance*, 1057.
67 Sir Henry J. Wood, *My Life of Music* (London, 1946), pp. 228–9.
68 *Comoedia*, 12 April 1909.
69 Debussy, *Correspondance*, p. 617.
70 Ibid., p. 999.
71 Louis Laloy, *La Musique Retrouvée 1902–1927* (Paris, 1928), pp. 166–7.
72 In the recording of the set Debussy made for the Welt-Mignon piano rolls in 1913, he perfectly captures a slight sense of technical precariousness.

4 Something New, Which Surprises Even Ourselves

1 Claude Debussy, *Correspondance: 1872–1918*, ed. F. Lesure and D. Herlin (Paris, 2005), p. 2162.

2 Claude Debussy, *Monsieur Croche et Autres Écrits*, ed. François Lesure, 2nd edn (Paris, 1987), p. 310.

3 Debussy, *Correspondance*, p. 1952.

4 Ibid., p. 1851.

5 Debussy, *Monsieur Croche*, p. 311.

6 Debussy, *Correspondance*, p. 1468.

7 Debussy, *Monsieur Croche*, p. 30.

8 See David J. Code, 'Parting the Veils of Debussy's "*Voiles*"', *Scottish Music Review*, [Online] 1/1 (December 2007), pp. 43–67.

9 Pierre Boulez, *Orientations*, ed. Jean-Jacques Nattiez, trans. Martin Cooper (London, 1986), pp. 318–20.

10 Debussy, *Correspondance*, p. 1253.

11 Ibid., p. 1316; François Lesure, *Claude Debussy: Biographie Critique* (Paris, 1994), p. 328.

12 Debussy, *Correspondance*, p. 1366.

13 Jacques Durand, *Quelques Souvenirs d'un Éditeur de Musique* (Paris, 1924), p. 124.

14 Debussy, *Correspondance*, p. 1331.

15 Ibid., p. 1341.

16 Ibid., p. 1373.

17 Ibid., p. 1384.

18 Ibid., p. 1384. He mistakenly thought Maud Allan was English.

19 See Robert Orledge, *Debussy and the Theatre* (Cambridge, 1982), p. 217.

20 Debussy, *Correspondance*, p. 1335.

21 Ibid., p. 1339.

22 Debussy, *Monsieur Croche*, p. 317; p. 324.

23 Debussy, *Correspondance*, p. 1445.

24 *Comoedia*, 18 May 1911.

25 Debussy, *Correspondance*, p. 1418.

26 Debussy, *Monsieur Croche*, p. 327.

27 Louis Laloy, *La Musique Retrouvée 1902–1927* (Paris, 1928), p. 207.

28 Lesure, *Claude Debussy*, pp. 341–2.

29 *Le Matin*, 23 May 1911.

30 Robin Holloway, *Debussy and Wagner* (London, 1979), p. 158.

31 Debussy, *Monsieur Croche*, p. 327.

32 Debussy, *Correspondance*, p. 1415.

33 Orledge, *Debussy and the Theatre*, p. 230.
34 Holloway, *Debussy and Wagner*, pp. 147–9.
35 Orledge, *Debussy and the Theatre*, p. 232.
36 Debussy, *Correspondance*, p. 1433.
37 Ibid., p. 1437.
38 Ibid., p. 1445.
39 Ibid., p. 1464.
40 Ibid., p. 1471.
41 Ibid., p. 1300; p. 1503.
42 See Jean-Michel Nectoux, ed., *Nijinksy: Prélude à l'après-midi d'un faune* (Paris, 1989), pp. 21–3.
43 Ibid., p. 20.
44 See the Interview of 23 February 1914, quoted in Lesure, *Claude Debussy*, pp. 350–51.
45 See the review by Gaston Calmette in *Le Figaro*, 30 May 1912, reprinted in Nectoux, ed., *Nijinsky: Prélude à l'après-midi d'un faune*, p. 47.
46 Debussy, *Correspondance*, p. 1760, n. 1.
47 Debussy, *Monsieur Croche*, p. 243.
48 Debussy, *Correspondance*, p. 1555.
49 Ibid., p. 1540.
50 Ibid., p. 1531.
51 See Herbert Eimert, 'Debussy's *Jeux*', trans. Leo Black, in *Die Reihe*, v (Bryn Mawr, PA, 1961), pp. 3–20, at pp. 19–20.
52 Debussy, *Correspondance*, p. 1619; p. 1758.
53 Jacques-Émile Blanche, 'Un Bilan Artistique de la Grande Saison de Paris', *Revue de Paris*, 1913. Reprinted in his *Dates* (Paris, 1921), pp. 139–82, at p. 171.
54 Lesure, *Claude Debussy*, p. 365.
55 Debussy, *Correspondance*, p. 1554.
56 Ibid., p. 1609.
57 Georges Jean-Aubry, 'Debussy et Stravinsky', *Revue de musicologie*, XLVIII (1962), p. 109.
58 Igor Stravinsky et al., *Avec Stravinsky* (Monaco, 1958), p. 23.
59 Debussy, *Correspondance*, p. 1687.
60 Debussy, *Monsieur Croche*, p. 210; p. 215.
61 Guido Gatti, 'The Piano Works of Claude Debussy', *Musical Quarterly*, VII/3 (1921), pp. 418–60, at 422.

62 Ibid., p. 445.
63 See for example Richard Cándida Smith, *Mallarmé's Children: Symbolism and the Renewal of Experience* (Berkeley, CA, 1999).
64 Debussy, *Correspondance*, p. 1667.
65 Ibid., p. 1651.
66 Ibid., p. 1662. For the parodic references see Orledge, *Debussy and the Theatre*, p. 182.
67 Debussy, *Correspondance*, p. 1651.
68 Ibid., pp. 1707–8.
69 Ibid., p. 1717.
70 Lazare Saminsky, 'Debussy à Petrograd', *La Revue musicale*, I/2 (1 December 1920), p. 216.
71 Quoted in Debussy, *Correspondance*, p. 1723, n. 3.
72 Debussy, *Monsieur Croche*, p. 156.
73 Ibid., p. 263.
74 Debussy, *Correspondance*, pp. 1767–8.
75 Ibid., p. 1824.
76 See Orledge, *Debussy and the Theatre*, pp. 248–9.
77 Debussy, *Correspondance*, p. 1836.
78 Ibid., p. 1842.
79 Ibid., p. 1843.
80 Ibid., p. 1911.
81 The reference is to Vincent d'Indy. See ibid., p. 1947.
82 Ibid., p. 1947; p. 1952.
83 See for example the pamphlet by Camille Saint-Saëns, *La Germanophilie* (Paris, 1916).
84 Debussy, *Correspondance*, p. 1850.
85 Ibid., p. 1854.
86 Ibid., p. 1847.
87 Ibid. p. 1863. For the Baudelaire reference see 'Les Petites Vieilles' in *Les Fleurs du Mal*.
88 Frédéric Chopin, *Valses*, ed. Claude Debussy (Paris, 1915), p. ii.
89 Cited in Debussy, *Correspondance*, p. 1879, n. 2.
90 Ibid., p. 1888.
91 Ibid., p. 1904.
92 Ibid., p. 1917.
93 Ibid., p. 1915.

94 Ibid., p. 1916.
95 See for example Marianne Wheeldon, *Debussy's Late Style* (Bloomington, IN, 2009), pp. 43–54.
96 Debussy, *Correspondance*, p. 2093.
97 Ibid., p. 1947.
98 Claude Debussy, *Douze Études pour le Piano* (Paris, 1915), ii.
99 Debussy, *Correspondance*, p. 1943; p. 1948; p. 1953.
100 Ibid., p. 2023.
101 Ibid., p. 2071.
102 Ibid., p. 2016.
103 Ibid., p. 1960.
104 Ibid., p. 1997.
105 Ibid., p. 2033.
106 Darius Milhaud, *Notes sans musique* (Paris, 1949), p. 77.
107 See Wheeldon, *Debussy's Late Style*, pp. 40–43.
108 Debussy, *Correspondance*, p. 2076.
109 Ibid., p. 2093.
110 Ibid., p. 2105.
111 Ibid., p. 2132.
112 Ibid., p. 2133.
113 *La Gazette de Biarritz*, 15 September 1917, quoted in ibid., p. 2146, n. 5.
114 Ibid., p. 2140.
115 Ibid., pp. 2161–5.
116 Ibid., p. 2160; p. 2166.
117 Camille Saint-Saëns and Gabriel Fauré, *Correspondance: soixante ans d'amitié* (Paris, 1973), p. 108.
118 Laloy, *La Musique Retrouvée*, p. 228.
119 Durand, *Quelques Souvenirs*, pp. 90–91.

Epilogue

1 Jean Cocteau, *Le Coq et l'arlequin: Notes autour de la musique* (Paris, 1918), pp. 27–8. Published in September 1918, the pamphlet was actually written before Debussy's death, and dedicated to the composer Georges Auric on 19 March.
2 Henry Prunières, ed., 'Numéro Spécial consacré à la mémoire de

Claude Debussy', *La Revue musicale*, I/2 (December 1920).

3 André Suarès, 'Debussy', in *La Revue musicale*, I/2 (December 1920), p. 99.

4 Suarès, 'Debussy', p. 112; Robert Godet, 'Le Lyrisme Intime de Claude Debussy', in *La Revue musicale*, I/2 (December 1920), pp. 167–90, esp. p. 180 and following.

5 Godet, 'Le Lyrisme Intime', p. 189.

6 Suarès, 'Debussy', p. 106.

7 Alfred Cortot, 'La Musique de Piano de Claude Debussy', in *La Revue musicale*, I/2 (December 1920), pp. 127–50, at p. 131.

8 Ibid., p. 132.

9 See Richard Taruskin, *Stravinsky and the Russian Traditions: A Biography of the Works Through Mavra* (Oxford, 1996), pp. 1459–62 and 1486–99.

10 See Richard Taruskin, 'A Myth of the Twentieth Century: *The Rite of Spring*, The Tradition of the New, and "The Music Itself"', in his *Defining Russia Musically: Historical and Hermeneutical Essays* (Princeton, NJ, 1997), pp. 360–88.

11 Pierre Boulez, *Relevés d'Apprenti* (Paris, 1966), p. 336; Jean Barraqué, *Debussy*, 2nd edn, ed. François Lesure (Paris, 1994), esp. pp. 191–4.

12 Claude Debussy, *Correspondance: 1872–1918*, ed. F. Lesure and D. Herlin (Paris, 2005), p. 1201.

13 Ibid., p. 2163.

Select Bibliography

Musical Scores

Detailed information about autograph sources can be found in James R. Briscoe, *Claude Debussy: A Guide to Research* (London, 1990). The Durand edition of the *Oeuvres complètes* has been in preparation since 1985, first under the direction of the late François Lesure, latterly under Denis Herlin. So far, the piano, orchestral and stage works have been published in full or in part. A useful supplement is Briscoe's two-volume critical edition *Songs of Claude Debussy* (Milwaukee, WI, 1993). See also Margaret G. Cobb, ed., Richard Miller, trans., *The Poetic Debussy: A Collection of His Song Texts and Selected Letters*, 2nd edn (Rochester, 1994).

Letters and Critical Writings

Debussy, Claude, *Correspondance: 1872–1918*, ed. François Lesure and Denis Herlin (Paris, 2005)
—, *Letters*, ed. and trans. François Lesure and Roger Nichols (London, 1987)
—, *Monsieur Croche et Autres Écrits*, ed. François Lesure, 2nd edn (Paris, 1987)
—, *Debussy on Music*, ed. François Lesure, ed. and trans. Richard Langham Smith (London, 1977)

Iconography

Gauthier, André, ed., *Debussy: Documents Iconographiques* (Geneva, 1952)
Lesure, François, *Claude Debussy*, Iconographie musicale (Geneva, 1975)

Debussy's Life and Music

Abbate, Carolyn, '*Tristan* in the Composition of *Pelléas*', *19th-century Music*, v/2 (1981), pp. 117–41

Austin, William, ed., *Claude Debussy: Prélude to 'The Afternoon of a Faun'*, a Norton Critical Score (New York, 1970)

Barraqué, Jean, *Debussy*, 2nd edn, ed. François Lesure (Paris, 1994)

Bergeron, Katherine, 'Mélisande's Hair, or, The Trouble in Allemonde: A Postmodern Allegory at the Opéra-comique', in *Siren Songs: Representations of Gender and Sexuality in Opera*, ed. Mary Ann Smart (Princeton, NJ, 2000), pp. 160–85

Boulez, Pierre, *Relevés d'Apprenti* (Paris, 1966)

Code, David J., 'Debussy's String Quartet in the Brussels Salon of *La Libre Esthétique*', *19th-century Music*, xxx/3 (Spring 2007), pp. 257–87

—, 'Hearing Debussy Reading Mallarmé: Music *après Wagner* in the *Prélude à l'après-midi d'un faune*', *Journal of the American Musicological Society*, LIV/3 (2001), pp. 493–554

—, 'Parting the Veils of Debussy's "*Voiles*"', *Scottish Music Review* [online], I/1 (December 2007), pp. 43–67

DeVoto, Mark, *Debussy and the Veil of Tonality* (New York, 2004)

Dietschy, Marcel, *A Portrait of Claude Debussy*, ed. and trans. William Ashbrook and Margaret G. Cobb (Oxford, 1990)

Eimert, Herbert, 'Debussy's *Jeux*', trans. Leo Black, in *Die Reihe*, v (Bryn Mawr, PA, 1961), pp. 3–20

Emmanuel, Maurice, *Pelléas et Mélisande de Claude Debussy*, 2nd edn (Paris, 1950)

Fulcher, Jane, ed., *Debussy and his World* (Princeton, NJ, 2001)

Gatti, Guido, 'The Piano Works of Claude Debussy', *Musical Quarterly*, VII/3 (1921), pp. 418–60

Holloway, Robin, *Debussy and Wagner* (London, 1979)

Howat, Roy, *Debussy in Proportion: A Musical Analysis* (Cambridge, 1983)

Joos, Maxime, ed., *Claude Debussy: Jeux de Formes* (Paris, 2004)

Jullien, Adolphe, 'Théâtre national de l'Opéra-comique: *Pelléas et Mélisande*', *Le Théâtre*, LXXXIV (June 1902), pp. 5–15

Kerman, Joseph, *Opera as Drama* (New York, 1952)

Laloy, Louis, *Claude Debussy* (Paris, 1909)

Lesure, François, *Claude Debussy: Biographie Critique* (Paris, 1994)

Liebich, Louise, *Claude-Achille Debussy* (London, 1908)
Lockspeiser, Edward, *Debussy: His Life and Mind*, 2 vols (London, 1962)
Marnold, Jean, 'Les "Nocturnes" de Claude Debussy', *Le Courrier musical*, v/5 (1 March 1902), pp. 68–71
Messager, André, 'Les premières représentations de *Pelléas*', *La Revue musicale*, VII/7 (1 May 1926), pp. 112–13
Mueller, Richard, 'Javanese Influence on Debussy's *Fantaisie* and Beyond', *19th-century Music*, x/2 (1986), pp. 157–86
Nectoux, Jean-Michel, ed., *Nijinksy: Prélude à l'après-midi d'un faune* (Paris, 1989)
Nichols, Roger, *Debussy Remembered* (London, 1992)
—, *The Life of Debussy* (Cambridge, 1998)
—, and Richard Langham Smith, *Claude Debussy: Pelléas et Mélisande* (Cambridge, 1989)
Orledge, Robert, *Debussy and the Theatre* (Cambridge, 1982)
Parks, Richard, *The Music of Claude Debussy* (New York, 1979)
Pasler, Jann, 'Debussy, *Jeux*: Playing with Time and Form', *19th-century Music*, VI/1 (1982), pp. 60–75
Peter, René, *Claude Debussy*, 2nd edn (Paris, 1944)
Pierné, Gabriel and Paul Vidal, 'Souvenirs d'Achille Debussy', *Revue musicale*, VII (1 May 1926), pp. 10–16
Priest, Deborah, *Louis Laloy (1874–1944) on Debussy, Ravel and Stravinsky* (London, 1999)
Roberts, Paul, *Claude Debussy* (London, 2008)
—, *Images: The Piano Music of Claude Debussy* (Portland, OR, 1996)
Schaeffner, André, *Essais de musicologie* (Paris, 1980)
Smith, Richard Langham, 'Debussy and the pre-Raphaelites', *19th-century Music*, v/2 (1981), pp. 95–109
—, ed., *Debussy Studies* (Cambridge, 1997)
Suschitzky, Anya, 'Debussy's Rameau: French Music and its Others', *Musical Quarterly*, LXXXVI/3 (2002), pp. 398–448
Thompson, Oscar, *Debussy: Man and Artist*, 2nd edn (New York, 1967)
Trezise, Simon, *Debussy: La Mer* (Cambridge, 1994)
—, ed., *The Cambridge Companion to Debussy* (Cambridge, 2003)
Vallas, Léon, *Claude Debussy: His Life and Works*, trans. Maire and Grace O'Brien (Oxford, 1933)
Vallery-Radot, Pasteur, *Tel était Claude Debussy* (Paris, 1958)

Vuillermoz, Emile, *C. Debussy* (Paris, 1957)
Wenk, Arthur, *Claude Debussy and the Poets* (Berkeley, CA, 1976)
Wheeldon, Marianne, *Debussy's Late Style* (Bloomington, IN, 2009)

Context and Contemporaries

Baudelaire, Charles, *Oeuvres complètes*, ed. Claude Pichois (Paris, 1975–6)
Berlioz, Hector, *Grand traité d'instrumentation et d'orchestration modernes* (Paris, 1843)
Blanche, Jacques-Émile, *Dates* (Paris, 1921)
Boulez, Pierre, *Orientations*, ed. Jean-Jacques Nattiez, trans. Martin Cooper (London, 1986)
Carré, Albert, *Souvenirs de théâtre*, ed. Robert Favart (Paris, 1950)
Clark, T. J., *The Painting of Modern Life: Paris in the Art of Manet and His Followers* (Princeton, NJ, 1984)
Clive, H. P., *Pierre Louÿs (1870–1925): A Biography* (Oxford, 1978)
Cocteau, Jean, *Le Coq et l'arlequin: Notes autour de la musique* (Paris, 1918)
Code, David J., 'The Formal Rhythms of Mallarmé's Faun', *Representations*, LXXXVI (Spring 2004), pp. 76–119
Davis, Mary E., *Erik Satie* (London, 2007)
Dukas, Paul, *Correspondance*, ed. Georges Favre (Paris, 1971)
—, *Écrits sur la musique*, ed. Gustave Samazeuilh (Paris, 1948)
Durand, Jacques, *Quelques Souvenirs d'un Éditeur de Musique* (Paris, 1924)
Favre, Georges, *Compositeurs français méconnues* (Paris, 1983)
Fulcher, Jane, *French Cultural Politics and Music: From the Dreyfus Affair to the First World War* (Oxford, 1999)
—, *The Composer as Intellectual: Music and Ideology in France, 1914–1940* (Oxford, 2005)
Indy, Vincent d', *Cours de Composition Musicale*, ed. Auguste Sérieyx and G. De Lioncourt (Paris, 1948–57)
Laloy, Louis, *La Musique Retrouvée 1902–1927* (Paris, 1928)
Lavignac, Alfred, *Le Voyage Artistique à Bayreuth* (Paris, 1897)
Lehning, James R., *To Be A Citizen: The Political Culture of the Early French Third Republic* (Ithaca, NY, 2001)
Louÿs, Pierre, *Milles lettres inédites de Pierre Louÿs à Georges Louis 1890–1917* (Paris, 2002)

Maeterlinck, Maurice, *Le Trésor des Humbles*, 42nd edn (Paris, 1904)
Mallarmé, Stéphane, *Oeuvres complètes*, ed. Bertrand Marchal (Paris, 1998)
Maus, Madeleine Octave, *Trente années de lutte pour l'art: Les XX et La Libre Esthétique 1884–1914* (Brussels, 1926)
Milhaud, Darius, *Notes sans musique* (Paris, 1949)
Millan, Gordon, *Pierre Louÿs ou le culte de l'amitié* (Aix-en-Provence, 1979)
Ravel, Maurice, *Lettres, Écrits, Entretiens*, ed. Arbie Orenstein (Paris, 1989)
Rolland, Romain, *Richard Strauss et Romain Rolland: Correspondance, Fragments de Journal* (Paris, 1951)
Saint-Saëns, Camille, *La Germanophilie* (Paris, 1916)
—, and Gabriel Fauré, *Correspondance: soixante ans d'amitié* (Paris, 1973)
Sanson, Rosamonde, *Les 14 Juillet (1789–1935)* (Paris, 1976)
Signac, Paul, *D'Eugène Delacroix au néo-Impressionisme* (Paris, 1899)
Smith, Richard Cándida, *Mallarmé's Children: Symbolism and the Renewal of Experience* (Berkeley, CA, 1999)
Stravinsky, Igor, et al., *Avec Stravinsky* (Monaco, 1958)
Taruskin, Richard, *Stravinsky and the Russian Traditions: A Biography of the Works Through Mavra* (Oxford, 1996)
—, *Defining Russia Musically: Historical and Hermeneutical Essays* (Princeton, NJ, 1997)
Wood, Sir Henry J., *My Life of Music* (London, 1946)

Select Discography

Vocal-Orchestral and Stage Works

L'Enfant prodigue (with Arthur Honegger, Symphony no. 3)
Jeanine Micheau, Michel Sénéchal, Pierre Mollet, Coro e Orchestra Sinfonica RAI di Torino, conducted by André Cluytens. Arts Archives 43059–2. Recorded 1962.

La Damoiselle élue (with the *Nocturnes* and *Le Martyre de Saint Sébastien*, symphonic fragments)
Dawn Upshaw, Paula Rasmussen, Women of the Los Angeles Master Chorale, Los Angeles Philharmonic Orchestra conducted by Esa-Pekka Salonen. Sony SK 58952. Recorded 1993.

Rodrigue et Chimène (ed. Richard Langham Smith; orch. Edison Denisov)
Donna Brown, Lawrence Dale, Hélène Joussoud, José van Dam, Jules Bastin, Vincent le Texier; Lyon Opera Chorus and Orchestra conducted by Kent Nagano. Erato 4509–98508–2. Recorded 1993–4.

Pelléas et Mélisande
Anne Sofie von Otter, Wolfgang Holzmair, Laurent Naouri, French National Orchestra conducted by Bernard Haitink. Naïve V4923. Recorded 2001.

Pelléas et Mélisande
Claudine Carlson, Collette Alliot-Lugaz, Didier Henry, Françoise Golfier, Gilles Cachemaille, Montréal Symphony Orchestra and Chorus conducted by Charles Dutoit. Decca 430 502–2. Recorded 1990.

Pelléas et Mélisande (DVD)
Alison Hagley, Neill Archer, Donald Maxwell, Kenneth Cox, Penelope Walker, Samuel Burkey, Peter Massocchi, Orchestra and Chorus of Welsh National Opera, conducted by Pierre Boulez. Videotaped at the New Theatre, Cardiff, March 1992. Deutsche Grammophon 073 030–9. Recorded 2002.

Le Martyre de Saint Sébastien (incidental music)
Leslie Caron, Sylvia McNair, Ann Murray, Nathalie Stutzmann, London Symphony Chorus and Orchestra, conducted by Michael Tilson Thomas. Sony SK 48240. Recorded 1991.

Le Martyre de Saint Sébastien (concert version), with *Trois Ballades de François Villon* (orch. Debussy)
Bernard Plantey, André Falcon, Claudine Collart, Jeannine Collard, Christiane Gayraud, Choeurs et Orchestre de la Radiodiffusion Française, conducted by Désiré-Émile Inghelbrecht. Testament SBT 1214. Recorded 1955, 1957; remastered 2001.

Songs

Forgotten Songs: Dawn Upshaw sings Debussy with James Levine, piano. Includes the early 'Vasnier songbook', the *Ariettes oubliées* and the Baudelaire songs. Sony SK 67190. Recorded 1995.

Debussy: Mélodies
François Le Roux with Noël Lee, piano. Includes most of the later cycles, the *Proses lyriques*, and various early songs. Le Chant du Monde. Released 1999.

Nuits d'étoiles: Mélodies françaises (with songs by Fauré and Poulenc)
Véronique Gens with Roger Vignoles, piano. Includes *Fêtes galantes I* and the *Chansons de Bilitis*. Virgin Classics 545360 2. Recorded 1998–9.

Maggie Teyte: Mélodies (with songs by Duparc, Berlioz and Fauré)
With Alfred Cortot and Gerald Moore, piano. Includes both *Fêtes galantes*,

the *Chansons de Bilitis*, the Baudelaire songs and the *Proses lyriques*. Pearl GEMM CD 9134. Recorded 1936 and 1940.

Orchestra

Debussy: Orchestral works (2 disc set)
Royal Concertgebouw Orchestra, conducted by Bernard Haitink and Eduard Beinum. Philips Classics 00289 438 7422. Recorded 1992.

Debussy: Nocturnes, La Mer, Prélude à l'après-midi d'un faune
Chicago Symphony Orchestra, conducted by Sir Georg Solti. Decca 436468. Released 1992.

Debussy: Orchestral Music (2 disc set)
New Philharmonia Orchestra and Cleveland Orchestra, conducted by Pierre Boulez. Sony SM2K68327. Recorded 1966–8.

Piano: solo, four hands, two pianos

Claude Debussy: The Composer as Pianist.
Includes six *Préludes*, one *Estampe* and *Children's Corner*; plus an excerpt from *Pelléas* and three songs with Mary Garden. Pierian 0001. Welte-Mignon piano roll recordings, 1904 and 1913; released 2000.

Estampes, Images, and *Préludes* (2 disc set)
Claudio Arrau. Philips Classics 432 304. Released 1991.

Complete Works for Solo Piano (2 volumes)
Jean-Yves Thibaudet. Decca 4520222 and 4602472. Released 1996 and 2000.

Preludes (I), Images (I and II), Children's Corner
Arturo Benedetti Michelangeli. Deutsche Grammophon 413 450–2 and 415 372–2. Recorded 1971 and 1978.

Etudes, Michuko Uchida
Decca The Originals 4757559. Recorded 1989.

Images, I and II; Etudes
Pierre-Laurent Aimard. Teldec 8573839402. Released 2003.

En blanc et noir (with works by Bartók and Mozart)
Martha Argerich and Stephen Kovacevich. Philips 476 7938. Recorded 1977.

Chamber Music

Debussy: Musique de Chambre (All the main works, including several for piano 4 hands and 2 pianos)
Christian Ferras, Pierre Barbizet, Maurice Gendron, Jacques Février, Michel Debost, Yehudi Menuhin, Lily Laskine, Quatuor Parrenin, Annie Challan, Michel Béroff, Jean-Philippe Collard, Orchestre de la Société des Concerts du Conservatoire conducted by André Cluytens. EMI Classic CMZ 67416. Recorded 1962–82.

Debussy, Ravel: Chamber Music (Includes the incidental music for the *Chansons de Bilitis* and Ravel's Mallarmé songs)
The Nash Ensemble, with Delphine Seyrig and Sarah Walker. Virgin Classics 5614272. Recorded 1989–90.

Quatuor à cordes en sol mineur, op. 10
Quatuor Ébène. Virgin Classics 5190452. Recorded 2008.

Piano trio in G major (with trios by Ravel and Fauré)
Florestan Trio. Hyperion CDA67114. Recorded 1999.

Acknowledgements

I am grateful to the British Academy and to the University of Glasgow's John Robertson Bequest for grants in support of this publication. Thanks also to Vivian Constantinopoulos at Reaktion Books for commissioning the book and for her editorial suggestions; to Harry Gilonis and Martha Jay for their help with illustrations and copy-editing; to Bill Sweeney for facilitating some valuable teaching release at an early stage of writing; and to Katherine Bergeron for her ongoing support. The book is dedicated to Nic, with love and thanks.

Photo Acknowledgements

The author and publishers wish to express their thanks to the following sources of illustrative material and/or permission to reproduce it.

© ADAGP, Paris and DACS, London: p. 9; photo akg-images/Erich Lessing: p. 6; photo author: p. 9; photos Bibliothèque Nationale de France, Paris: pp. 57, 58, 65, 66, 87, 157; from *Le Charivari*, 1868: p. 38; photo Glasgow University Library (Special Collections): p. 72; photos Lebrecht Music and Arts Photo Library: pp. 16, 23, 26, 89, 100, 109, 123, 147, 149, 154; photo Library of Congress, Washington, DC (Prints and Photographs Division - Harris & Ewing Collection): p. 115; Musée de la Musique, Paris: p. 6; Musée National du Château, Versailles: p. 30; photo The Pierpont Morgan Library, New York: p. 137; photos Roger-Viollet/Rex Features: pp. 14, 30, 38, 71, 104, 116, 128, 152, 177, 188.